Praise for V‹

M000044493

"*Voices of the Grieving Hear*‹
profoundly compassionate fri‹
sharing the heavy load of sorrow, letting anyone of any age living through
any sorrow know, they are not alone. We will never be alone."
Naomi Shihab Nye
Young People's Poet Laureate, Poetry Foundation

"Grief shatters our hearts. These poems vividly convey the compassion and
the courage that can bear this brokenness. Let their tender strength heal
you."
Dale Borglum
Executive Director, Living/Dying Project

"In forty-five years of providing support and intervention to grieving
individuals, families, responders and the community, I have found that the
voice of poetry more accurately describes the nuance and depth of the grief
journey than volumes of text. Mike Bernhardt, out of his own experience,
has gathered these seeds of honest pain and redemptive beauty. *Voices of the
Grieving Heart* will heal and open your poetic voice to the true gift."
Janet Childs
Founder and former Director, Centre for Living with Dying

"The grieving process following the death of a loved one often defies words
to describe our inner feelings. The writings in *Voices of the Grieving Heart*
capture what many of us have felt but have not been able to put into words.
Reading this book was a deep, moving and important healing experience for
me." *(From preface of first edition)*
Jerry Jampolsky
Author of *Love is Letting Go of Fear*

"*Voices of the Grieving Heart* by Mike Bernhardt is a beautiful book. It will
touch you deeply, move you to tears and heal you. Read it and awaken to
life." *(From first edition)*
Bernie S. Siegel, M.D.
Author of *Love, Medicine and Miracles*

"These are the articulations of the grieving heart. Each poem is a perfect
mirror, an encouragement to heal. This is the poetry of our joy and
exhaustion, living and dying with the consequences of love. This is our voice
when our heart is broken." *(From first edition)*
Stephen Levine
Author of *Who Dies* and *Meetings at the Edge*

"At the edge of the mystery of death, we offer the poetry of our truth into the silence." *(From first edition)*
Ram Dass, Spiritual Teacher
Author of *How Can I Help?* and *Walking Each Other Home*

"Poetry is the song of the soul. *Voices of the Grieving Heart* captures these soul songs and collects them into a poignant, comforting, and healing volume for those suffering from the loss of a loved one. I was immediately drawn in and am richer for the reading. You will be too."
Gary Roe, Award-winning author, speaker, and grief specialist
Author of the *Comfort for the Grieving* series of books

"This beautiful book speaks directly to the heart with moving and powerful poetry from people who generously share their journeys of love, loss, healing, and hope. If you are grieving the loss of someone you love, it will help to validate your experience and feelings. With a section devoted to grieving in the time of pandemic, and an invitation to experience the healing power of writing through your own grief, it is as personal as it is universal."
Debbie Augenthaler, LMHC, NCC
Author of *You Are Not Alone*

"In an age where grief is made more complex by pandemic isolation, *Voices of the Grieving Heart* embraces readers within a healing community, where one hears their own voice emerging from the words of others."
Joe DeSantis, Chaplain
Samaritan Life-Enhancing Care

"I am grateful Mike Bernhardt had the resilience, strength, and clarity to collect the poems in *Voices of the Grieving Heart*. I would have loved to find this gem during my early months of grieving. These poems realize, poignantly, the form of witnessing that poems take on, and help to connect us to others like us as we navigate our deep grieving."
Prageeta Sharma, Henry G. Lee Professor of English at Pomona College
Author of *Grief Sequence*

"The voices in *Voices of the Grieving Heart* are healing voices, voices that have kept company with grief, voices that reflect the deep sorrow and trajectory of mourning from trying to let go, to holding on, to letting go, again and again. Mike Bernhardt has meticulously gathered poems that speak to the complexity and singularity of grief. This is an essential book that I plan on gifting time after time to friends and family who have lost loved ones."
Georgia Heard
Poet, Writer, Teacher, and Inventor of Heart Maps®

"Here are voices that tell us not *what* to feel, but how *they* feel, speaking from the deep places touched by grief and love. Anyone who has lost a loved one will benefit from the honest, courageous, and generous sharing found in these pages."
Elizabeth Bremer, MA, LMFT and bereaved spouse

"Within the lovely pages of *Voices of the Grieving Heart*, you will find profoundly poignant expressions of unimaginable sorrow. However, companioning the sorrow, you will find hope for healing and a new tomorrow."
Vicki Smith, LMFT
Grief Counselor, Hospice of the East Bay

"*Voices of the Grieving Heart* will be a benefit in helping counselors better understand the feelings and thoughts of those who grieve. I recommend it to other professionals and volunteers who work with the grieving."
Mona Reeva, L.C.S.W., M.P.H.
Former Director of Grief Studies, John F. Kennedy University

"Before there was 'self-help' literature, there was literature—those works that heal because they are from the heart. *Voices of the Grieving Heart* is a work of art that speaks directly to the soul, from the real experts—those who have experienced death, grieving and healing. For us who are tired of being told what we're supposed to feel, *Voices of the Grieving Heart* offers a refreshing truth about the transformative power of loss and pain." *(From first edition)*
Stephanie Ericsson
Author of *Companion Through the Darkness: Inner Dialogues on Grief*

"*Voices of the Grieving Heart* repeatedly calls us to face the mystery of life and death. I strongly recommend this work for anyone who is ready to open the deepest realms within." *(From first edition)*
Ronald Valle, PhD
Director of Awakening: A Center for Exploring Living and Dying

VOICES of the
GRIEVING HEART

Edited by Mike Bernhardt

Cypress Point Press
Moraga, California

https://cypresspointpress.com

VOICES OF THE GRIEVING HEART
Second edition
Copyright © 1993, 2021 by Mike Bernhardt

Cover design by Matthew Félix
https://www.matthewfelix.com

Author photograph by Yvonne Lefort

Library of Congress Control Number: 2021900552
ISBN 978-0-9642810-1-1 (paper)
ISBN 978-0-9642810-2-8 (ebook)

*For Susan,
whose deathless love
inspired this book—
her gift to me,
and mine to her.*

*And for all of the contributors:
this book only exists
because of your voices.
Thank you.*

A Note to the Reader

The sections of this book follow, more or less, the path of grieving *as I experienced it*, which is to say that they only partially coincide with the stages we are so often told our grief "should" follow. In general, we all move from the shock and agony of *The Raging Storm* toward, hopefully, a sense of the presence of *The Breath of Great Spirit*. But everyone grieves differently. I am not implying that your grief journey should follow a particular map.

You may find at any given time that one section will resonate for you far more than the others, or a particular poem will inspire you. You may also find that some poems say exactly what you don't want to hear—even poems which previously inspired you. What is cathartic one day may be uninteresting the next. What presently seems pointless may become profound a few months from now. Grief is a non-linear process. So feel free to bounce around the book.

Some of the poems in this book may elicit a strong emotional response. That is one of the goals of this book—to help you identify and express what you are feeling. However, if your grief is very fresh, try not to read too many poems at once. At such fragile times, we sometimes don't realize that we have taken in too much until we suddenly find ourselves overwhelmed. Take your time. You may even want to talk with a counselor or therapist to help you work with the feelings that arise as a result of your reading.

The authors and artists in this book contributed their works in the hope that they might help you heal, as their creative expression helped them to heal. Perhaps this book will inspire you to express yourself creatively as well—if so, there is section in the back to keep your own poems. And when you are unable find the words to speak the depths of your own heart, I hope it will be a resource for you, a place to sit and know that you are not alone.

Table of Contents

Acknowledgments

Hundreds of pieces of poetry and artwork were submitted to me from all over the USA as well as from Europe, Australia, and India. So many were beautiful, heartbreaking, and healing. I am honored and grateful to have been trusted with the heart and poetry of every single person who sent me their work, whether their submissions were ultimately included or not.

One contributor who deserves special thanks is Cassandra English. In the first edition, she contributed two drawings that came out of the losses she'd experienced. This time, she created four new pieces at my request, on short notice. She drew on her own heart's voice, yet somehow knew exactly what I was looking for with little input from me.

I can't thank John Fox and the Institute for Poetic Medicine enough for his support in helping to make this book everything I hoped it would be, including the foreword he wrote, which I have frequently described as "stunning."

Thank you to Claudia Olivos and Olivos Art Studio for generously letting me use her gorgeous artwork on the book cover, and to Matthew Félix for designing the cover.

The late Jerry Jampolsky encouraged this project when it was little more than a hopeful dream. His supportive words and deeds were gifts at a time when I truly needed them, and I'm saddened at his recent passing.

Finally, thank you to my wife Yvonne, the woman behind my throne. For thirty years, she has supported and loved me. In the early nineties she gave me space as I continued to grieve the death of my first wife. In 2020, she convinced me that I had to publish this second edition. She brainstormed ideas, proofread and copy-edited a million versions, and marketed the book with her exceptional networking skills. She never lost my vision for this project, even when I did. I am a lucky man.

Preface to the Second Edition

Today is the 30th anniversary of the day my first wife, Susan, died. I've thought many times over the years about republishing this book since its initial release in 1994. The time never seemed quite right. Now, it is.

As I write this, the world is still gripped by the COVID-19 pandemic. Over a half-million people have succumbed in the United States, millions worldwide. And because of isolation protocols, even those with unrelated illnesses are dying alone in medical facilities every day. Families are left in anguish, unable even to see their loved ones, let alone kiss them goodbye. The normal rituals and tools of mourning—sitting shiva, holding a wake or memorial, even hugs—are currently fraught with danger. Grief is isolating enough without "social distancing" and the sterility of our new, contact-free world.

The pandemic will pass. Eventually, people will gather in person again, and we will find comfort in mourning and honoring our loved ones together. But long after most of our friends and coworkers have moved on with their own lives, those of us who have lost someone we loved still will likely be walking the path of grief, alone. I hope that this book will be like having someone to walk with; someone who *knows*.

Regarding this new, expanded edition:

I reconnected with most of the contributors to the first edition of this book to ask them where they are now, thirty years later, in relation to the losses they'd experienced. The responses of many of them, and in some cases their recent poetry, are in a new chapter called *Time Passes*.

I also put out a new call for poetry submissions and received many, many responses. This new edition has twice as many contributors and poems as the original. There is a new chapter called *Pandemic*, containing poetry that deals with the grief, isolation, and unique hardships caused by the world in which we live right now. Many new poems have been added to the other sections as well.

Lastly, I added a new section in the back, on page 269—an invitation to you, the reader, to write your own poetry. There are some suggestions to get you started, and blank pages to keep your writing. I encourage you to add your own voice to the community gathered on these pages.

Mike Bernhardt
Moraga, California
April 7, 2021

Foreword by John Fox

Poetry enacts our own losses so that we can share the notion that we all lose—and hold each other's hand, as it were, in losing.

—Donald Hall

I welcome you to this book, *Voices of the Grieving Heart*. You are holding in your hands something that shows you what it means to be a human being. Contained herein are bone thoughts. Yes, each poem goes deep.

However, I feel it is my responsibility to give you fair warning. Perhaps the word *warning* isn't the best—because I don't mean you ought to be frightened. At any given vulnerable time, it's true, a word like *warning* when it comes to grieving, could be appropriate for you. I say be kind to and gentle with yourself then—light a candle, lick an ice cream cone, listen to a favorite piece of music.

I'll use another phrase I just thought of—if not a warning, this book is a "hearts-up." That is, these poems are definitely not a heads-up—another way to suggest warning. In these pages, the steady-going head has slipped on the ice, slipped on the incline of wet moss, slipped on the proverbially unexpected, unseen banana peel. In these poems, the head is falling down into the heart.

That is why these poems are here at all. That's what they do.

The word *grieving* is what matters. "Grief" alone sounds static and dry. *Grieving* is what a person does over time. You could say it is what they are as they walk around or try to sleep, as they breathe or even try to breathe. Even more, like a river, grieving connects us to so much else including much that is underneath and, up to now, unsaid.

One thing is for sure. Grieving gets the person who slips

down from head to heart very thoroughly wet. Consider the times you have fallen into a wet-making current of grieving.

On a spring day in 1976, when I was twenty years old and attending Bard College, I walked towards the student center, Kline Commons. Sitting on the grass in front was a circle of people. Speaking to that circle of people was Elisabeth Kübler-Ross, the woman renowned for opening America to a profound consideration of death and dying. I knew some about her work.

It's been my way to respond to opportunities. This was one! I told Elisabeth that two years prior, my right leg was amputated below the knee. Since the age of four and a half, I had made it through life with seven surgeries and many hospitalizations. I didn't tell her that last part; I am telling you, dear reader.

Dauntless as I could act much of the time while growing up, the honest truth is that at that time, on my own in college, I was hiding what I truly felt: shame, fear, isolation. I kept up a good front but inside, losing my leg was a huge loss. In many ways I myself *was* that loss. Sitting in that circle, I sunk into grieving.

Elisabeth insisted (demanded?!) that I attend a five-day workshop she was offering that summer in Halifax, Nova Scotia. A few months later, I went. There, without a single wasted moment in those five days, I experienced what Naomi Shihab Nye writes in her poem, *Kindness*:

Before you know kindness as the deepest thing inside,
you must know sorrow as the other deepest thing.
You must wake up with sorrow.
You must speak to it till your voice
catches the thread of all sorrows
and you see the size of the cloth.

During those days I saw the size of the sorrow cloth. It wasn't really bad, and it wasn't good. Instead, it totally blew my mind. I felt, saw and listened to human beings come alive in their most vital, real and true being. I can say LIFE opened up during those days.

Yet I haven't told you about myself during that workshop. Elisabeth Kübler-Ross, small of stature, was like a hawk. As quick as lightning, she could dive upon her prey. Before striking she didn't give one a chance to get upset. The moment she turned to look at me, sitting on couch at the side of the room, she said, "Come here and sit down." I did. She was curled up on a small couch with room for two.

Then she told me to take off my pants and remove my prosthetic leg. In doing what she said, I slipped big time and in my underpants at that. Instantly, I was wet in my grieving and all that accompanied it.

Elisabeth had that intense, hawk-like aspect; yet she was compassionate. Her compassion wasn't idiot compassion, or rather more nicely put, like a Hallmark card for grieving. Her compassion was fierce.

She knew what Gerald Jampolsky (the writer of the foreword to the first edition of *Voices of the Grieving Heart*) knew—love is letting go of fear. This wasn't just a wise, comforting thought to think about. In that moment—this letting go was FOR REAL. Elisabeth invited forty people in that room to approach me and *touch my stump*.

I don't think I have ever been as frightened in my life. Yet I had never been so loved. What a paradox. It meant something to me that I was being loved by so many others who, I knew, had themselves gone through, or were going through, hell.

My grieving didn't end then. But that experience of being touched with great care had a growing place in me. Even today, I bow to Elisabeth again and again.

This renewed edition of *Voices of the Grieving Heart* that Mike Bernhardt has lovingly gathered, curated in his very moving and thoughtful way, is exquisite. Yes, his choosing to republish it to honor the thirtieth anniversary of his wife Susan's death is beautiful. But I feel to do this in the midst of this god-awful pandemic, in these multiple seasons of raw grieving—this necessary, bold act is heroic.

I trust that by reading a single poem, you will touch that poem and the person who wrote it. Your reading, considering, and feeling will touch the poem and the person who wrote it with loving awareness.

The surprising thing might be for you to discover that, like me having my stump touched, like that poet who willingly takes you down to their bone thought, you too are nearly naked in whatever grieving you live with. That's the fair warning, that is the hearts-up. Take what Donald Hall said as true: this book is someone's hand—and you are holding it.

I invite you to allow that poem, that person to touch you with loving awareness. What is community and a flourishing heart if not something so real, so wet, so true?

John Fox
Mountain View, California
March, 2021

Voices

Poetry born from the pain of grieving
inseparable from the pain of growing
Death creating life
a flower blossoms from your fertilizer
Muse! Brother! One and the same
Your spirit ever present gives me courage to write
We talk in the land of dreams, I rejoice
knowing you continue to live
Our poems a testimonial to your existence

Mara Teitel Sheade

Introduction

Grief is a tidal wave that overtakes you, smashes down upon you with unimaginable force, sweeps you up into its darkness, where you tumble and crash against unidentifiable surfaces, only to be thrown out on an unknown beach, bruised, reshaped... It is the ashes from which the phoenix rises, and the mettle of rebirth. It returns life to the living dead. It teaches that there is nothing absolutely true or untrue...

Grief will make a new person out of you, if it doesn't kill you in the making.
—Stephanie Ericsson, from *Companion Through the Darkness*

My wife Susan died unexpectedly in April 1991, the Sunday after Easter. I could never have imagined beforehand how transformative an experience that would be. Nothing was true anymore but the truths of her death and my continued existence. I was shaken to my foundations, forced to decide what I would keep of myself and what I would throw away. Every aspect of my life was subject to review, from my occupation to my spiritual beliefs, from my choice of friends to my choice of doctors.

Although some friends were very supportive, for about a year I also attended a weekly grief support group at the Center for Attitudinal Healing. I needed to spend time with people who knew how uncontrollable and consuming grief could be, who wouldn't ply me with explanations, consolation and helpful advice. One of the guidelines of our group began with the words, "We recognize that love is listening." I wanted to be listened to, and to hear other people's stories as well.

Social niceties seemed pointless, and I gradually discarded some people from my life. I just could not bear the thought of having to relate to someone with whom I wasn't deeply bonded. I let my voicemail answer the telephone so I didn't have to speak to anyone, and I sometimes erased messages without even listening to them first. An acquaintance left a delicious tuna salad on my doorstep—because I made believe there was no one home when she knocked. Though I appreciated her gift, I never thanked her or even spoke to her again.

Psychologists have defined the stages of grieving; different models of grief provide different names for them. However, there are no stages when we are in the middle of our grief. There is only what we are feeling NOW. I could move from sobbing to a sense of peace to sobbing again in a matter of minutes. Sometimes I was terrified of pain, but more often of numbness. Occasionally, I hoped that a truck would accidentally run me over and kill me. For months afterwards, the shock of Susan's death would unexpectedly hit me over the head, even as I slowly began to look forward with hope. Sometimes I would get mad at myself for this "backward slide." I have since come to understand that nothing was wrong with my progress—only with my useless attempts to analyze it.

I needed answers to so many questions: Why did she have to die? What was I going to do with the rest of my life? How could I, alone, even keep up with our friends and the chores of daily living? I was forced to learn to stay in the present. I got better, as the poet Rainier Maria Rilke wrote, at "living the questions," letting go and allowing the answers to come in their own time rather than searching for them too much. "Trust yourself" became almost like a mantra for me. I learned how to listen to my heart and to my intuition.

I began writing the day Susan died: keeping a journal, writing poetry, trying to document and express my grief and my transformation. It was the first time I'd done any writing in many years. Sometimes poetry was the only way to give words to the overwhelming emotions I struggled with. In finding that I could express my feelings creatively, I discovered a whole side of myself that had been lying dormant. Writing gave me a new sense of strength and wholeness. Now when I look back, reading my poetry and journals, I can see how far I have come and remember what I went through. Doing that from time to time seems to have a healing quality of its own.

I wanted to read about others' experience but found little published material that interested me. I understood my grief from the inside; I didn't want to be "taught" about grief and the transformation I was going through. I couldn't concentrate on long texts anyway, and often got bored after the first few pages. I yearned for honest experience and validation rather than guidance. *Voices of the Grieving Heart* grew out of my desire to publish something for people who felt the same way I did.

This book is a collection of poetry that shares the pain, growth, changes, healing and gifts that can come when people we love die. The contributors are from every walk of life. Several are respected writers with a list of publishing credits; a few had never written poetry before. Originally, I viewed this book as a project for my own healing and for the benefit of those who would read it. I soon learned that for many contributors, sending me their work was an important part of their healing as well. I received some very moving letters from people who opened up to me as if we had known each other for years. Several contributors told me that I was the first to read the poems they had submitted to me, but that they knew this book would be a good place for them.

In order to give words to an experience so personal and powerful as grief, we have to make ourselves very vulnerable. I believe that is where the healing begins—in being willing to open up and feel the sadness, the joy, the agonizing pain, the numbness, guilt, the losses and gains, all of it. Trust your heart. Take the time. Grief is an open wound that only festers when we ignore it. The miracle is that in opening to our pain, however long it takes, we can become more whole than when we started.

I would never have begun, let alone completed, a project like this if I were still the person I was before Susan died. In her death I found the gift of my own life. In my grief I found a greater ability to love. May this book also help you to find the gifts that lie hidden in your pain, and may you find the courage to live your new life as fully as you can.

Mike Bernhardt
December, 1993
Moraga, California

Someone Died Today

No matter how prepared or unprepared we are for death, no matter how old or young we are, no matter how much we say "I love you," no matter how "good" or "bad" a death it was, no matter how relieved or anguished we feel, no matter what our spiritual or religious beliefs are, the death of a loved one shocks us with its finality. They are gone forever from this world, and our lives will never be the same.

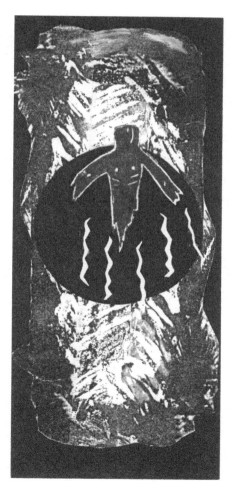

Sunday

Together, we survived the terrifying night
of CPR and defibrillation, too many tubes and wires and
   doctors,
my kisses on your forehead and your eyes kissing me back
until your EKG exploded and they told me to leave.
I sat outside in the hallway talking softly with you.

In the morning, though your eyes seemed empty,
I expected your recovery and went home to sleep
only to be greeted by a ringing phone and an urgent voice
and I was out again, stuck in traffic on the Bay Bridge,

praying, screaming at God to get me to you in time.
Hoping that curses and prayers might be enough,
I inched and fought my way through traffic and despair
until finally free, nearly drowning

I plunged into the streets racing
to San Francisco General. Sometimes now
I like to imagine what I would have told the police
if they'd noticed. I like to think that I wouldn't have
    pulled over

I would've just plummeted on at
70 miles per hour up Potrero Avenue letting
them catch up to me in the parking lot as
I ran inside MY WIFE'S DYING! I would've screamed

but they didn't notice.
I ran inside alone
to find my friends crying
and you, dead.

Mike Bernhardt

Robert's Death

Sunday afternoon
and your room is filled with light,
white light forged from all the rainbow.
Your face is pain from a day and a night
without one good breath; your voice,
a rasp rubbed between two pillows.

There you are, crawling backstroke
through the searing desert, parched for water;
water like a last-ditch mantra
before your vision of afterlight
breaks through the dam of sunlight
flooding daylight with nightlight.

Present in the moment of passage,
you are more real than the portent dream of yourself,
more light than forty years should bring,
more ready to travel than the Bactrian camel,
more a home for who I am
than I have ever known.

It is your last hour; the sound of your breath
is like air filtering through water,
bubbling to the surface,
bursting into light like flashbulbs in my ear;
your last hour, longer than life, slowing time,
slowing down between each breath, slowing.

I can feel Allen's presence with us in the light,
beckoning, opening his arms.
You turn and look up into Victor's eyes.
What do you tell Victor in your eyes?
I can see such light, glinting, reverberating,
looking for the light's way out, looking

on past Victor into Allen's ghost-lit eyes,
breath slowing; will there be another? no,
and then a breath; your face eases, slowing,
will there be another? slower, no, and then a breath;
slow, no, and then, no. The old eyes
change color from green to gray blue.

Almost instantly, you are not here,
you do not linger:
I cannot taste any of you in the air, just light.
You and Allen have linked arms, traveling out.
I want to hold too, but I let go.
You are so light.

Sam Ambler

Someone Died Today

Someone died today.
My brother died today.
He died of AIDS.
People do die, you know.
It wasn't nothing.
It wasn't a mere blip on the screen.

It was a gruesome, horrific death.
Painful and shocking to witness.
Skin drawn so tight over his skeleton
that his eyes would not shut.
And then there was the dementia.
Was that Matt
or was that some distortion?
I never knew.

He said that he was lost.
He asked if he were alive or dead.
Where is the white light, I wondered?
Please, God he needs YOUR help!

He was 29.
Handsome once.
An athlete once.
A fisherman once.
An alcoholic.
A human being.
A teacher of harsh realities.
An inspiration.
A hero for many.

I shed tears today.
My heart was broken today.
It shall mend, but
it wasn't nothing that
my brother died today.

Elizabeth Kuykendall

Cameo

Here was the gathering of the family
In the peeling yellow hospital room

It was your birthday. It was the last time.
We brought our gifts, our offerings:

Abalone - pearl and blue rivers of heaven;
Eau de Cologne to dab on your forehead

Coconut sweetmeat, a fold-out wonky zebra
your favourite psalm in my best handwriting.

You, father, the warm heart of us
you, the protective circle around us

Striving to stay, straining to leave, your face
full of distance, distracted with pain

We didn't know you were already
losing the horizons of flesh and time.

Now it is we who have broken open
a river of perfume flows between us.

No words, no endings to recall
only this stark cameo

All of you and all we would become
comprehended in this relief

White silhouette raised upon the dark
your gift, the remembrance of love.

From there walking out forever
into shifting and unknown ground.

Rosemary Palmeira

Until the Milk Stops

Day 1
Engorged breasts, waiting to feed.
Their last fare was midmorning
and routine. It is evening;
two feedings have been missed.
A few hours earlier, the lifeless child
was pressed against these breasts,
but they could not understand.

There is no pill to stop the flow,
not now. Relief comes only
by expressing the milk.
After a few days, it will stop.

The cold plastic pump
sucks the milk painfully.
There is no let down,
the breasts fight to release their nurture.

The milk is collected in sterile bags,
frozen out of habit and for what?
After months of saving every drop
for the frail child, it is impossible
to pour it down the drain.

Day 3
These breasts ridicule me.
Theirs was the only milk she would take,
yet
it would not sustain her.
This ritual—a morbid reminder
I could never do enough.

Day 4
There is no more to express.
The breasts are limp
and dried up,
the emptiness complete.

Lorene Jackson

Tunnel's End

I didn't call you back
   when your empty eyes
   filled with death's color.

I could have pleaded
   for you to stay
   but I didn't call you back.

Did you hear
   when I breathed
   against your ear
   a repeated refrain:
   "I love you?"

My voice traveled with you
   through the gray tunnel
   stretching its walls
   like beckoning arms,
   and seduced
   you moved forward.

I didn't call you back,
   swallowing those words
   to house them forever
   in an unreachable crypt.

Pauline K. Schmookler

Quiet Rooms

(Editor's note: Sarah and Rita, co-authors of this piece, performed this poem live on several occasions, with Sarah reading the left-hand part in a measured voice and Rita reading the right-hand part emotionally. The fourth line from the end is read by both of them together.)

They have them now,
quiet rooms,

"I can't feel anything.
No kicks."

a place to bury stillborn dreams

"Find the heart beat."

between our swollen breasts.

"Find It!"

Quiet rooms,
where soundproof walls
protect us

"What are you waiting for?"

from the lusty cries
of newborns,
pink and hungry for their lives.

"What's wrong?"

(continued)

Quiet rooms
where there is no quiet,

                "What are you doing?"

where trembling fingers
cannot touch the shrouded eyes,

                "Speak to me!"

and sobs can breathe no life.

                "She *isn't* dead."

Quiet rooms.
Two days to touch

                "Give her to me."

the blue tinged feet
and perfect fingers,

                "I want to see my baby."

a place to cuddle,

                "Give her to me!"

and gently wrap
our little ones
against the chill.

                "They've taken my baby away,
                wrapped in paper."

Quiet rooms,
a private place
to share with him,

                "Where are your tears?"

to place on film
the unproud moment
of our lives,

> "When will we forget,
> to remember,"

and kiss
unsuckled lips
before they turn to wine.

> "the face we never saw?"

Quiet rooms,
a place to nurse our babies,
dead before they have lived.

> "An unmarked grave.
> No place to go."

We still have them.

They have them now,
quiet rooms.

> "Too late for me."

Sarah Rossetti and Rita La Bianca

My Father's Arms

The moment was so very quiet.
His last breath came and went.
I watched, transfixed,
unable to move.
Listening. Listening.
Hoping for his
breathing to resume.
Watching for the
rise and fall
of my sweet father's chest.
It had ceased.
The life force whispering its retreat.

I witnessed my father's passing.
From this life to the next.
An eternal moment recorded
in time, space,
a transitory shift
in the particle-wave matter
of my father's existence.

Three, maybe four hours later,
men from the morgue
came to take my father.
Sounds emanating,
grief, disbelief,
No, No, No,
pacing,
movements violent
yet supple,
collapsing inward,
as if somehow such frantic pleas
would reverse the reality,
the finality.

Phone calls.
To family, friends.
Arrangements.
In a haze.
The gentle passing of a tender soul.

Debra Ann Halloran

Etched in My Brain

Face down on the bed, my son,
arms outstretched and legs grown cold.
One tainted pill, did you in
at twenty-four years old.

I quickly turned you over
and looked deep into your eyes.
"He's gone!" I screamed. "He's gone!
    He's gone!"
with anguished, high-pitched cries.

I peered into your open mouth
with vomit on its side
and horror overtook me then
as part of me had died.

I ran around the kitchen
like wounded, helpless prey.
I cursed out loud then whimpered some
when they took you away.

I carry this, etched in my brain
and guilt, since last I checked,
a father's job is to love
but mostly to protect.

Ken Slesarik

Brother

We're in shock,
Floundering about in a wilderness of platitudes and
    epitaphs,
'Cause you've gone tramping and left us behind.
Is this our life now?
Beating ourselves up with woulda, coulda, shoulda?
You knew through and through that love is compassion,
But didn't offer enough of it to yourself.

Your kooky shrill laughter at the absurdities of life will
    never leave me.
Good men are driven by a desire to do good,
And great men are driven by their flaws.
You were good and great, brother, in equal measures.
You were frugal about saving and generous about love,
In all the right ways,
Always striving to be a better partner and father.

Didn't you know, you were always,
And I mean always,
Enough?
What the fuck are you doing dead?
Did you feel like a burden?
Like the world is a better place without you in it?
You never were,
And it isn't.

Sarah Rossetti

Words I've Never Said

I have never said the words I now have to say.
My brother died today,
At 7:22 a.m., May 9, 2020.
I wasn't there at Holy Name Hospital Hospice
When it happened,
Nor am I there a day later,
My first day without him.
Covid-19 made sure of that.

I am having difficulty
With simple decisions,
And the order of things.
What's proper protocol,
What's necessary?

There's a certain civility in silence
That carries me today.
I wander to the patio
To look at the
Japanese azalea I got at CVS yesterday.
Plants are strong medicine.
Its trunk is beautifully braided and strong.

I will get a proper pot
For it so it can
Stay firmly planted
On the patio
Until it's ready
For the heat of the outdoors.

I don't want to rush
Its body being released
To the soil.

It gives me peace to see it,
A physical representation
To mark persistence of life,
Because of or in spite of
The marching of time.

The minute details
Will happen when they do.
Meanwhile, the steady song
Of rain dripping from
Sky,
To roof,
To flower petals,
To ground,
Surrounds me in a sacred
Snapshot
Of calm.

Deborah Eve Grayson

The Call

In the half dark of a summer night
air hangs heavy as I lie listening
to my father's rhythmic breathing,

unprepared for the shrill shock
of the sudden call.

Aeons later,
bird song heralds a dawn
I cannot believe you will not see.

A strange sun rises in an alien sky;
an unfamiliar world ahead.

Gill Garrett

Last Winter

Late in this, your sixty-eighth winter
your blood counts continue to fall—
like the snow just outside your window,
but softer, quieter, and
more devastating.

I see no fear in you, nor
even resignation,
just the simple acceptance of
the stages of life which rooted
so deeply in you as a farm girl.

Your sons gather around in your last hours.
"Well," you say, as calmly as if finding
some nice tomatoes in the garden, "it sure has been
a great life knowing you guys."
We never received a greater gift, and surely never will.

But as you slip away,
the crocuses you loved so well—
brilliant yellow, white, and lavender—
poke their heads above the snow,
harbingers of the new Spring.

Michael Frachioni

The Way It Wasn't

I would have sat
forever at your feet,
and listened to the stories
you loved to tell—

like the one
about 5 year old me
counting coins
on the liquor store floor
to see if I could afford
a pack of gum
for my mother.

It's the way you saw my heart
I might miss the most.

I always pictured us together
at the end, crossing
the sacred bridge-space
between breath and no breath,
granddaughter caring for
grandmother now:

anointing your feet
with lavender oil, in awe
that they carried you
all 94 years;

separating your soft,
white hair into braids,
adorning your neck
with the pearls you
always wanted;

singing your three
favorite hymns,
serenading you
into the next world,
the way you once sang
your babies to sleep.

I would have held
your hands
until they went cold.

Instead, I woke
to a voicemail
that you had
passed that night
during the thunderstorm.

Shannon M. Pace

The Raging Storm

Emotions tumble over us—intolerable pain, rage at our loved one, ourselves and God, terror about the future, depression thick and black, joyous release, love deeper than we thought we could ever feel, or a quiet numbness, an emptiness in which we can feel nothing at all. We may fear we are going crazy. We may move from the heights of transcendence to the depths of despair—or vice versa—in moments. We know now what it means to have a broken heart. We don't know if we will survive it.

After the Service

Where I stood and
nervelessly
   eulogized my brother
my voice not breaking once—
not even once—
while my mom and sisters
   wept so helplessly
a man comes to shake my hand,
to tell me what a terrific job I had done.
He says to me:
   I hope you take the time to grieve, yourself.

I look at him dazedly.

It is impossible to describe
   this grief
to anyone.
I could say
   I was in mourning, that
I was grieving my loss,
but what sentence
would hold the description of the form grief
takes now:

the gasping, hyperventilating sense
   of it,
the bending over at the waist while simultaneously

beating
my breast with closed fist,
the howling—
   UHHHHH UHHHHHHHHH—
that is so loud and fierce—
even with my head buried in a pillow—
that
I am somewhat surprised the neighbors
haven't called the police.

Or the way my heart hurts with such an angry,
   desperate, pounding cadence
that I want to reach into my chest cavity and
rip it out.
I smile blankly at the man
   a stranger
and assure him I do.

Nori J. Rost

Mother is Dead

She's dead
She's dead
My inner voice speaks

I rush to her side
Her lips are blue
Her face is cold
A fly is humming

I scream and scream
After thirty years
I scream.

Monica Jean Davis

The Struggle Inside

Today I pretend to smile
My fingers push the corners of my mouth
Yet my eyes tell no lies, bearing still fresh
The pain of your death.

In two days you are one month gone
Yet time moves outside my domain
I bite my lip so others will not know
The raging storm inside my soul.

You could have told me
Just once to let me know
I, racked with sleepless nights
Afraid to dream yet still afraid to wake.

The truth is so empty now.
I watch couples wander by, so easy to notice
Their simple tender ways of heart shaped caring
Developed over time.

Oh, God let me know that you are safe and filled with love
I breathe deep and feel my love of you
As I surrender again to the unknown
And stay wildly out of my mind.

Annie Brook

Loss of a Friend

words freeze tonight
and stick to my tongue
even the knocking on the door
goes hollow
like wings of lost birds
beating on the window glass

outside the street lights push me
into a circle of shadows
while I search strangers' faces
one by one frantic to find
someone I know

you have slipped into the dark
never turning back

Margaret Grote

Words

(for Jamie and Sarah)

What we know is that we know no words
for when the heart breaks or when it fails
to see the sun again. How do we hold
anything in our hands after the
gravity of emptiness? What keeps us
here on earth after love and memories
depart? What equation are we given
to solve? What answer now tests our
faith? Why so short this journey?
Where are the footsteps that should
be behind us? God teach us the language
only you understand. Tonight prayers
speak only tears.

E. Ethelbert Miller

Scream at the Ocean

The ocean waves pile up on one another
rolling forward relentlessly
smashing onto the beach
and eyes wide open, powerful in rage
I scream with all my might
but the surf drowns my voice

I cannot bring her back

Mike Bernhardt

Things I Want to Ask You
(In the Maze of the Minotaur)

Because who knows what happens
when we die?

I have always prided myself
        on my unknowing–
my claim that we are made of energy which
        never dies
but just
        goes on spiraling out into the vast universe;
as far away as the most distant star
you are

and perhaps
as close as the breath I just took in

and when I think of that
and imagine you here with me
swirling around in

        dust motes of regret
I want to ask you
was it worth it?

Are you satisfied with the outcome?

(continued)

Are you at peace?
> (this is the only question where I believe I know
> the answer

and   for that, anyway,
I am grateful.)

There are questions that haunt me
> In the darkest hours of night

when I awake
> And cannot sleep again

So I lie in bed,
> As tears stream down my face

and I ask you these simple things:
Are you happy?
Can you see the bigger picture now?
How much love this world held for you?
How much your presence meant?
> Do you see

from your broader perspective
that there were resources you could have used

that there was a way out of the minotaur's labyrinth
after all—

string to hold you fast to the light;

      do you see all these things now?

And will you promise me

promise me with all your shattered heart
that the next time you visit
this world
      in whatever form you take

that you will remember the thread
      the sword to kill the monsters in your soul
and return safely again
to the arms of those
      who love you?

Nori J. Rost

Early Mourning

The house stands sightless, blinded by death,
hushed into silence by unspoken words,
numbed by the cold hand of loss.

But after the ham is eaten, the whiskey drunk,
after the mourners emerge blinking
from its confines,

sensation will slowly, painfully return,
the pins and needles of a new normality.

Gill Garrett

Scream Dream

Squalls of Rage at those
Who didn't want to sit shiva for her disappearance
What could they say to exempt themselves from her
Stubbornness
Bewilderment
Lament
Refusal
Pain
Confusion
Attachment
Desire
Dismissal
Mad surrender
She only had a flash of brightness at my arrival
Was she sitting shiva for herself as
She abided by the custom?
No bathing
No pleasure
I could be unflappably tolerant at her bedside
But I scream at her in my dream

Margaret Wadsworth

The Last Visit

On this Saturday afternoon in July, my mother is alone.
Her body is being cremated right now.
I am not with her because no one thought I might want
   to be.
So, twelve hours after she died, I grieve alone.

It's odd doing this at home, no one with me.
My Dad, exhausted, rests at his house.
My three brothers are on different continents.
We are separated by beliefs wider than the land between us,
even if the space seems shortened by the staccato
of words uttered against metallic clangs, echoes across a
   sound barrier
no human voice ever could breach, a cell phone hell
that seems sacrilegious every day but especially today.
The snowblind braille of email offers another soulless option.
Either way there is no hand to reach for mine.

I weep alone, nobody here in the sunroom except
   the ficus tree.
The blinds cannot stop the sun from assaulting me
   through glass.

My Mother is also alone today. Instead of rays
through a double paned window, there are flames coming
   through vents.
Each of us, Mother, daughter, at this same moment,
lies perfectly still, absorbing heat, one the warmth of life,
   the other the fire of death.

I'm told it takes six hours. They started at 3 p.m.
so I will sit here in silence until 9 o'clock.
Though there is no *body* here, I will keep watch over it.
Though I'm miles away, I will be the wake.

I close my eyes. I am in that mortuary.
I observe the body glide into the flames. Instead of land,
   instead of sea,
my mother's burial is in fire. So I sit. It's the last thing I
   can do for her:
I bear witness.

Jill Jennings

Richard is Dead

Richard
     is
          dead.
The word sits
  on the page
like the obscenity it is.

Suzanne Fried-Freed

Sonnet for a Bereaved Parent

Lost is the image of the perfect child,
Held in that tender, blinding mother-love,
All-encompassing, soft and soothing as a mourning dove,
Now broken pieces scattered in the wild
And stormy seas of grief, piled
High, a load too heavy to be borne
By the breast from which perfection has been torn.
The world can never more be mild.

The image, fractured—how to regain the whole,
When everywhere is empty, vacant space,
Devoid of the once familiar face?
Here, pain and heartache reach one's very soul.
Raise high one's cry to heaven's Almighty Power,
That bitterness and pain shall not devour.

Elspeth Monro Reagan

How So?

Doing fine, he always said.
He phoned each week just like you should, on Sunday,
around eight. He never forgot like some.

Teaching at the college! Proud, oh yes I was proud.
I showed the pictures of the children, one named
after me. She has his smile, and mine.

Clean bill of health, not broke or stoned or out of gas.
Took care of his own just fine and even
sent me violets on my birthday.

How so...?
I cringe and shiver, slumped into that spidery corner
heart dripping blackest blood beside me.
Mother of a suicide.

Dixie Pine

For Aunt Bobbie

How can it be that I was measuring
rocks for a garden
while you were dying?
How can it be that I was chopping
vegetables, peeling onions
while you struggled to breathe?
How can it be I didn't know you
were suffering, or did I
not want to know?
How can it be I wasn't there
the way I'd always imagined
I'd be if you needed help
to live or to die?
I waited too long
to ask the questions
only you could answer.
They told me not to call to
tell you one more time
how much I loved you.
You took your last
breath while I slept,
unaware of you leaving.
How can it be you are gone
from this world and yet
I am still in it?

Dawn Nelson

Traces

no, No, NO as you lay dying. Defiance
practiced in two letters scatters bitter spores
everywhere now that you are dead. No! NO
splinters, pins me limp in our bed, merciless.

What was lost when you died dulls the sunlit glint
from the window, drifts dust behind the empty
woodstove. No skitters beside chairs and crouches
under the couch; No whispers and howls as choice

withers within quick pain's grip: Photos of you.
Worn T-shirts. Winter hats. The box where I found
your glasses. Day kicks ashes and grit. Silence
stings me sleepless. Midnight nothingness glistens.

Claudia McGhee

Ten Minutes Left

Ten minutes left in 1990
Zach died this year
My heart rhythm is erratic
Swiftly moving downstream—can't paddle backwards
Seven minutes
Now I'm getting desperate
Take me back to April 1990 I have to get there quickly
Before it's too late
Throbbing in my throat now, tears well up
I want my mommy
Zach COME HOME NOW RIGHT NOW I SAY
Don't let anyone hear you moaning
Four minutes left
I can hear fireworks outside
And the television shrills
It's almost over
Will walks in, kisses me, says Happy New Year
I'm alone now by request
At the New Year
Appropriately

Zach died last year.

Virginia Steele Felch

Missing Richie

There
the sorrow
sits
patiently
like   a   spider
spinning
   her
        web
soon
soon she whispers.

The knife
   falls
from
my
hand
rough clatters to the
                    floor.
i
sit
weeping
my dear dear brother
you are gone
how dare i be
happy?

Once again
the confusion falls
can't i have
both?
don'tknowdon'tknow...
guiltguiltguilt
       runs
deeply
in my heart
how breathe
with you dead?

Suzanne Fried-Freed

The Aftermath

Mother, I see the world through your eyes—
horror, fear, a world gone berserk.
Anguish and rage from over forty years ago.
I grieve for the millions dead, not just relatives
I never knew—my "grandfather," my "uncle"—
"Your middle name came from his," you used to say.

And I, daughter of a Holocaust survivor,
have never lived through a war
but I carry the memories with me:
of gas chambers, crematoria, sirens, Volkswagens,
Dr. Oetker's foods, old people in Bavarian cafés...
I carry it all with me.

I never wanted to see the world as you saw it—
Godless!
"How could there be a God if six million Jews died?"
Nobody who wasn't Jewish could be trusted—
Was he a Nazi?
Was his grandfather a Nazi?

You could never go back to Germany, your home.
"It used to be a beautiful country."
I long to have roots.
The world through my eyes does not seem real.
This is your pain, Mom,
and you're not alive anymore to take it back.

Yvonne Lefort

My Children Lost

I dream of them suckling my breast
I dream of them
So many babies, dead
How do I heal

I grieve
I cry
I yell
I scream at God
I leave my husband
who does not grieve

I hate my body
It is a barren thing
It cannot hold the seeds
It expels dead babies

I sob
I pray
I feel so empty
I feel so much anger

I talk to them
I tell them of my love for them
I wanted you
I will see you when I am called.

Monica Jean Davis

Daddy Love

Daddy Blue Eyes
Ocean of Love
Sun of my heart
Your touch—my warmth

The sun gone out
The ocean drained
No arms surround me
No eyes see me
This child can not yet see herself!
She can not yet hold herself!
Then where is she?
Then who is she?

No light
No warmth
Then who has died?
It must be me.

Victoria MacDonald

I Am Not Afraid to Die

I am not afraid to die.
I am just afraid of living...
and having to watch
everyone I love
one by one
get there before me.

Julie Hagie

Pandemic

Sometimes we had the chance to say goodbye. So many of us did not. Perhaps a nurse held a phone to our loved one's ear so we could say "I love you" one last time. We prayed that someone was holding our beloved's hand as death approached, learned of our loss from a phone call, or from an exhausted, masked, socially-distant doctor. Now we grieve alone, often unable to gather in traditional ways to mourn or celebrate our loved one's life. We gather on Zoom, or perhaps not at all. We wait for normalcy while knowing that without our loved one, life will never be normal again. We can't even cry in the arms of a friend without risking infection from a virus that has reached every corner of the globe.

To Hold the Loss

Before the pandemic losses,
the half million mark for America,
the global landscapes of loneliness,
the giving birth alone, the dying
alone, isolated ceremonies of loss
without the shoulder to cry on,
without the loaves of comfort offered
by the auntie, the neighbor, the friend,
I could turn my attention
to clamshells, pebbles,
the pleasures of sand underfoot,
the beautiful insignificance of my footprints,
and the metronome of the tides.

In this year of unspeakable loss,
like I once collected shells and stones,
I look for words to name this grief
that no pocket is large enough to hold.

Standing at this familiar beach,
I now look for seals, swimming
in our Northwest waters,
only to dream for a moment
that we might slip out of our skin
into something beyond us
where our shared grief might lodge.

What if we could submerge,
and learn to breathe under water?
Would it make our hearts larger,
would we learn to hold the losses
and breathe with them,
in the depths of this grief we share?

Merna Ann Hecht

Plastic-Covered Phone

You never spoke badly about anyone
except politicians and baseball scores
And I never heard you curse
except when someone cut you off in traffic
But you said to me on the phone that Wednesday
    afternoon
from your hospital bed, "This is fucked."
I could tell you were angry
I could tell you felt helpless
and confused

Your wife was on a ventilator with COVID
And, unbeknownst to you, you were next.
Alone and scared, I imagine you,
when the police had found you collapsed on the floor of
    your house
Alone and scared, I imagine you, right before they
    intubated you.
And all that time, I was the most helpless
We were locked down
You were so far away
New York was crawling with a deadly virus
we knew nothing about
And all I could do was wait from afar.
Wait, it turns out, wait for you to die.
Die alone.
Hopefully, alone but not scared.

My last words to you were rushed—
the doctor cut me off as she held her plastic-covered
    phone to your ear—
she had so many other patients to attend to.
Did you hear me? Did you know how far away this all felt?
A series of firsts for the mourning:
watching your funeral on Zoom
holding "virtual shiva"
saying kaddish over Facebook

It all came on like a tidal wave
We barely knew what the virus was called
And so many were dropping like flies
And then you both were gone.

Weeks later, when we came to the empty house, we found
    a box of surgical masks sitting on your front stoop.
A mere precaution, I'm sure you thought, as you ordered
    them on Amazon.
The irony of our hindsight, the hindsight they call 20/20—
    all of it is hindsight now.
We were once simply blind.

Now, we live in a new, crazy world
that you didn't get to see.
Maybe, in some way, you are the lucky ones.

Julie D. Strongson-Aldape

A Prayer for My Brother

That I was not
There when you died
Constricts like a knot

Your lungs afire
Singed to ruins
Of ground glass & despair

Our pact, now broken
Haunts like a nightmare, our
Double solitude, its token.

I want to pour the red
Wine aged over the broken
Years we shared

Into a cup: relive smiles
That light my soul
Like a lighthouse for miles

Pulsing in the core
Of a new star, faraway
In a black heaven's purr

No art to throat
The choky heartbreak:
Sorrow's rucksack & coat

I trail your ghost
Claim our past's sweet verve
And rue what's lost.

My heart still chimes
Blue notes, Augustan
Pining for lost times.

Chike M. Nzerue

The Havoc of a Single Year
(for my sisters)

It began as most any year,
like a river meandering across the
landscape with nary a care. Two
months in, the waters swelled, flood-
like, sweeping us over jagged rocks,
cold grey waters chilling to the
bone. Senior statesman, eldest of the
clan, our brother succumbed in month
three, pulled under, tumbled over smooth
rocks, unable to get a hand-
hold on roots, branches, anything that
might slow his relentless downstream passage.

Then came the virus that kept
us apart...locked down each in
our states, we adapted as best
we could. We FaceTimed, we
Zoomed, we learned the bitter lessons
of contact-free, of no hugs. Numbness
tugged like an undertow, after attempts
at cheers like cooking, game nights
endless Netflix bingeing. Hollow-eyed, skirting
the blue boundaries of bereft, we
wondered, what more might this cruel year ask? But

be careful the questions you pose, for you mightn't
like the answers, which came too
soon for our sister, clan matriarch,
mother to three little girls in

the long-ago, those three now slouching
toward old age and stunned by
her sudden departure, like baby birds
fallen from the nest, blue-lidded, cheeping
wildly for their mama to return,
to give them the lifelong sustenance
of her companionship, care and protection.
Strong swimmer that she was, unable

to fight the brutal current of
this year, of the succession of
years, her movements grew languid,
muscles relaxed as she gave up
the long-fought battle, moving slipstream
as we watched from the flood
banks with grief-etched faces, no time
to say goodbye, for even one last
hug. So we mourn, months three
and months eleven weighing heavy
as stones in the pocket, avoiding the
waters, seeking safety in we three.

Kathleen Browning

Cloak of Stars
(for Chuck)

After you die, with the air
still in pieces, someone says
holy. We sit (masked)
in the yard, not close together.

A hawk (red tail or broad wing)
glides above us,
circles and circles, pale
and magnificent,
not leaving.

Is it too soon
to stitch this together?
No it's begun, the ingathering

of stories and moments,
your broad smile and magnificent
love for your family, pride
on your face in every photo.

Your soul is so spacious
that we pull it around ourselves
like a cloak of stars.

Cathleen Cohen

Chet

Covid killed him
a gregarious neighbor
conversing often across our fence.
I didn't know him well
nor was I so inclined
casual acquaintance enough.

Suddenly Chet was gone
I shocked and saddened
not having tried harder to know him.
His wife Jackie remained next door
our only acquaintance the plants
I watered while they vacationed.
How to say I was sorry to someone I didn't know?

Then I felt again my own grief
my sister's suicide
grief shared with Jackie.
We are friends now she and I
walking together often
talking of the worlds we share.
She speaks of Chet.
I'm getting to know him better.

We grieve because we have loved.

Kitch Martin

At the Window

We hold our gaze a moment longer
than we should and I worry she sees
the tears brimming my eyes. I gently release
my hand from the clear, cold glass
and watch our palm prints fade.

She knows only her side of the pane.

Days turn to weeks, to months, now a year,
my name's not on the list, so I wait
for the orderly to wheel her to the window.
I kneel, dial, turn speaker on,
and notice my purple scrubs look like
cosmos or china aster, a violet ruffling
against winter's white leftovers.

She lifts the land-locked phone to her ear,
we exchange pleasantries until
she asks what I wish she'd stop asking.

"Yes, we lost another three today.
But it will be okay, there's a vaccine now."
I say with a smile that melts into my weary lips.
"We'll get to celebrate Christmas together soon."
I add while she returns my smile and jokes,
"Good news is presents are cheaper at
	after-Christmas sales."

Let's both hold on to our missing Christmas,
I think, and not to the missing
time, touch, medicine, machines,
to the missing
breaths, bodies, standards, safety.
Let's both hold on.

"I'll be back tomorrow," I tell her.
"I'll be right here," she says
as tears cloud her eyes.

I know only my side of the pain.

Maggie Mosher

Wish

The world wasn't as ugly as it is now
Yet.
The pandemic was still fresh,
The news important.
We trusted what seemed like the truth,
Listening at the edge of our ears
For details of the spread,
Trying to dampen the dread by
Chanting, "We are in this together,"
Shushing those that interrupted,
And hushing distant fears.

We felt the camaraderie
Of shared outdoor activities,
Doing the do-si-do of sidewalk sharing
while dog walking, running or conversing.

You were fading from present tense
Faster than grief had time to remember.
There was no way to know
You would not see the end of Spring.
I was too polite to intrude
With phone calls I knew you couldn't answer
And texts you would never see,
And—once or twice—
A picture with a caption or a joke.

I wanted to be there with you
Protect you,
Bring comfort,
Share space,

But it was already too late.
I felt your momentum avalanche,
Your spirit
Crumble,
The pieces scattering
Like the marbles we used to play with as kids
on the splintered, wooden floors.

I leaned into the silence of unknowing,
This new territory haunting and hollow,
Praying,
Begging,
For a wish to be granted.

But the darkness remained silent…
The genie
and the magical lamp,

Absent.

Deborah Eve Grayson

Not Here Without You

The thin, glass, automatic
hospital doors open and shut
behind me, the temperature
of the whirling wind
no longer perceptible.

Six feet away, with only
his eyes visible, I see
defeat. I make it through
his words, with a nod that I
understand, questions
I managed to form
about if you were in pain
if someone, anyone, was with you
in that moment when they wouldn't,
couldn't let me in.
He tells me your things
will be released in a week or two.
It's not things I want,
it's you.

I make it back
tear off my mask
and let it drop to the floor
knowing that this motion will not
lessen the lack of air in my lungs.

I walk straight
to my bedroom door,
alone, shut myself in
where I can let my jaw tremble,
teeth chatter,
and hot wet tears drip down
so small, insignificant,
not matching the size
of this feeling
like I am dying,
no, like I want to die,
but am stuck here living
without you what feels
more final than death.

Maggie Mosher

Bridal Bushes

In the pouring May rain, after the ambulance collected
    her body
from the healing house we had created together
    in November,
I watched the red brake lights for as long as I could
    see them.
Then I began to walk along the lilac-lined street.

I thought of her last days there with the hospice angels
and her sisters, where I was no longer welcome.
Thinking they could shield her from the outside world,
they prayed for an unlikely miracle.
But Glioblastoma seldom spares.

I picked a lilac stem and the smell transported me home to
Memorial Day gravesites and other deaths:
    Spirea and lilac bushes lined our alley, supplying us
    with the petals for our
    he-loves-me, he-loves-me-not games.
    I didn't know then that she-loves-me,
    she-loves-me-not would also be a possibility.

She did love me and then she forgot.
A parade of her old lovers streamed through her healing
  house before the pandemic hit.
She forgot each of them in turn, the most recent one first,
until only her first love and her family remained.
On our last FaceTime; she smiled weakly as she lay back
  on her pillow.
Her face was sallow and her brown eyes didn't smile
  with recognition.
She was polite, but tired.

It had begun to rain. I thought I heard the honking geese.
Looking up, I said, "The honkers! Sandy!" Maybe they
  were saying good-bye.
Maybe she remembered *them* and blew them kisses 'til
  the end.

Christie Mudder

Thomas J. Dorton

A high school
Basketball player
In a small town,
All-American guy

Went to Vietnam
Came home to silence
No fanfare, no thank you.

Traveling down the road of grief
Can be a long, silent journey
Of fallen comrades
Carried in his heart and soul

Retired Army, business owner
Truck driver, school bus driver
Supporting his church and community

Quiet, gentle soul
Brought smiles and laughter
To little children,
Hugs, encouraging words

Then Covid grabbed him
and wouldn't let go
He spent days alone in ICU

His loving wife and children
Couldn't be there
Depending on nurses for information

The bullets of Vietnam
Didn't stop him
The memories didn't either...
But Covid robbed a
Family, a community of
The finest super-hero

A community made better
Because of one ordinary man
Who did extraordinary things
Traveling life's road seventy-two years
In our hearts always, never forgotten
We're all just traveling down grief's road.

Shirley Thacker

Pandemic Funeral

There is no body, no casket, no roses
just a computer screen of faces
to say goodbye to you—

My cousin, the lanky boy
of my childhood, just a year older
a foot taller, bruised at the knee
quiet but kind, always kind.

How do we send you off?
Without a church, without hand holding,
without leftover soups and casseroles,
the rituals of our grief achingly unobserved.

We tell our stories, your stories
the sounds of our voices reaching
through the screens—
the way we touch each other
when we remember you.

Kirsten Porter

Silent Hypoxia

We sent him home
To recover in isolation
No fever, just crack bark cough,

Unseen, lungs full of spikes,
Primed for a siege—
Lung rattle hushed in sleep,

No preexisting condition,
Oxygen & carbon dioxide
Playing their game of dice.

I, the physician fooled
By his swan-like calm,
Read the tea leaves wrong—

Their love, still strong,
Its flowers pale & stale—
His wife's tears, his last tea.

Chike M. Nzerue

21st Century Fruit

It was strange and sorrowfully sweet
having to navigate my Daddy's dying
There was no crying—not right away, anyway
Only a crash-course in Relationship-Building
with Dr. Zoom and Nurse Skype in ICU.

Seven days in limbo my Daddy floated
Tagged Covid P.U.I. upon arrival
No visitors in, no patients out, They said
Dying alone his biggest fear…and yet
Our only chance for survival.

It was strange and sorrowfully sweet
bringing family together
while in quarantined recovery myself
Only two relatives allowed, They said, and only when
Death is imminent. Of course, I made Them tell me
exactly what that meant!

It was not a stroke of genius, nor a bout of
temporary insanity, but rather
an executive decision made
by a Night-Shift Guard who opted
for compassion—instead of isolation—for humanity.

Even then, never giving in to the notion of a solitary
    passing
Technology was the portal, the power of Love, the key
to guide both our Bravest and our Bedridden
through the scariest parts
To shift focus on our ability to transcend circumstance
    at will
regardless of health conditions...no matter how far.

Stretching time like saltwater taffy with a lurking bite
Strange and sorrowfully sweet is this unfamiliar fruit
But it did bring a Peaceful Passing to the season

...along with a most compelling urge to reboot!

Paco-Michelle Atwood

Goodbye

I say goodbye to my father.
See his face.
Whisper the words
He cannot hear.
In the intimacy of the exchange,
There is stillness.
The stillness of death.
The stillness of my sister
Holding her phone.
Gifting me with closeness
Denied by Covid.
Forcibly far,
Three thousand miles distant,
I am
Transported through her device,
In grief,
In love,
In pixels,
Present by proxy.
For his military burial,
I stand alone
In black,
Attending through the digital wormhole
in my dining room
To say goodbye.

Elizabeth McMahon

Bill

Hold on tightly to my hand, Bill
Your family cannot be with you
But I am here
I can see the fear in your eyes though you cannot speak
If only you could see behind my mask, you would see
    there are tears in mine
Hold on tightly to my hand, Bill
I will be your family
I will say soothing words and you will be comforted in
    your last moments.
Do not be afraid as you drift from this world to the next
Your legacy will live on in the hearts of those whose lives
    you have touched
Hold on tightly to my hand, Bill
I will not let go
I will not let go

Yvonne Ugarte

Swimming the Cathedral

1

Rings of sunglow ripple
all-around me as I glide
underwater,

listening—

from the wavering quiet:
echo of holy
presence.

2

Immersed and enfolded
I can remember now:

the young man in the sea-green scrubs
and N-95 mask whose eyes cast
quickly about the room
as if searching for another door
when the counselor asks
How is it going for you?

His words tumble, tumble
like waves breaking before the storm:
gasping for air, it's the 40-year-olds
gasping for air. That's when you
double-check everything that you do
because you know if you make a mistake
that could be you, beside him,
gasping too.

3
Finally, I come up for air,
mouth open wide as if accepting
all that is placed upon the tongue:
this is my life poured out for you.

Cyra Sweet Dumitru

But You Elude Me

At the deepest level, how can we accept the finality of our loss? We see our loved one in a passing car or walking in a crowd, and suddenly realize that it was merely a cruel trick of the mind. The next day it happens again, as real as the day before. Everything reminds us of the death. Wearily, we trudge through our lives. We struggle to remember the sound of our loved one's voice, we look at pictures, we spend time with friends or time alone, trying to forget how much we hurt, praying that we won't.

Mary and Me

I used to wonder what it would be like
to be
shadowed
by Mary Oliver.
She would quietly follow me
around
every day
and then
write a poem
about my life—
about the minutes
that just passed,
and the beauty that I missed
and the chaos I chose to see
instead.
But now I wish she could
plunge her curious hands
Into the inky darkness of
my grief,
swirling her fingers round and round
until she captured
the essence of it all
and then,

withdrawing her hands
dripping with my pain,
paint words—
like shadow puppets on the wall—
so moving
and delicate
and strong
and heart-breakingly true
that the unquantifiable anguish
would almost make sense,
and the searing, blistering
hot iron pain
would almost be beautiful
and I would almost
be glad to have experienced
that deep darkness.
Yet even Mary Oliver can take me
only
to almost.
And that's not quite far enough
to make this bearable,
no matter how good I try to be
or how many miles of desert I cross.

Nori J. Rost

Mistaken Identity

I thought I saw you the other day.
My heart beat like mad.
I followed you closely, praying
that I wouldn't lose you again.
I wanted to run right up—
hug you and tell you how much I missed you.
I wondered where you would say you had been?
If you would be glad to see me too?
But then you turned and looked—
only to leave me standing there
caught in the realization that this was
a case of mistaken identity.
Suddenly I felt my heart's refusal to
believe that you were ever gone to begin with,
and the numbness, God, the numbness.
So I went home, locked the door, crawled
into bed with your picture under my pillow,
and prayed—that when I woke up
this would all be just a dream.

Julie Hagie

Double Takes

It happens now and then:
some detail, known and loved,
captures my passing glance
and rolls away the stone.
But, on the second look
it's just your hair, walk, stance,
in some other's body
and memory returns.

I know I won't see You.
Yet I scan crowds; hoping,
yearning to feel again,
for even a moment,
that sudden quickening
of my everyday heart,
that special joy I felt,
always,
beholding You.

Carlin Paige Holden

But You Elude Me

I go over to your house once or twice a week
every week since you passed on.
I water your plants, open your mail,
talk on your phone, soak in your bathtub, wash
with your soap, dry in your towels, watch your T.V.,
smell your sweet clean on your sheets,
sleep in your bed on the spot where you died.

I sip your tea reclining in your living-room
wingback chair, stare out your plate-glass
window at your downtown skyline view,
listen to your music contemplating your statues.
I snoop through your boxes, scan your
college papers, toss them in your trash barrel.
I empty your closets, step into your clothes.

I give away your art that you so loved,
your stoneware dishes, your oak tables,
your caned-seat chairs, your pull-out sofabed,
your mountain of books, your classic silk ties,
your bank-drag suits, your shoes and leather
boots, leather chaps, clamps, rings, sex toys,
your chatchkes, your shirts, socks, pants.

I take it all down; I give it all away: I give it
to your friends; I give it to strangers; I give it
to your parents and your beloved sister;
I give it to myself. I look at it all; I throw it all
away. Because you kept it I want to save it
too. I want to hoard everything;
I can't hold on to anything.

I drive your car. I drove screws through extra
locks on all your outside doors. I wired timers
on your porch light and the torchére
in your bedroom. I consult with your lawyer
and hire a lesbian realtor to help me sell
your house. I cry for you. I want you back.
I cannot feel you in any of it. I continue...

Sam Ambler

Eulogy for My Father

I feel a poverty
that makes the ordinary
disdainful and your leaving artificial.
I spin here, waiting,
on this wheel of grief
collecting the vouchers of the wake
as your gifts of love unfurl
into this illusion of night.

Our yesterdays
lack the miracle of remembrance;
your hand busy
making change into change,
never one to be held,
buried there in your pocket.
I believed in dreaming then,
it was dreams that I found.

Your barren lover is finally
free to embrace me:
I meant to tell you
that there is a comfort for me
knowing I am more than nothing.
As the wheel slows to stillness
anonymity remains your true legacy;
the only gift left to be opened.

David C. Burke

Thoughts While on Hold to the Florist

Mama died today.

At least "mama" is what they all called her,
My wife's family—nieces, great-grandchildren—
And she not really mama to any of them:
Maybe they're just calling her "dead" too...

And why should it matter
To me who didn't know her,
Except that Aunt Svea died yesterday
And her forbidden attic,
And her pearl necklace, and her library
On rainy Thanksgiving afternoons
Are still as sharp to me as her carving knife.
Oh, no one else I ever knew
Really had a cookie jar

And suddenly I am surrounded by death

Carrying my father's ashes in my arms;
Forgetting my sister's laugh, so long ago,
But remembering her little white coffin.

Norman Wendth

Where Will I Send the Roses?

When your sister is gone, who will *really* worry about
    your broken arm
and then remember you with your first Wiffle ball and bat,
your untamed hair emblazoned in sunlight,
    slender shoulders

swinging for the fences? Who will see your incandescence,
who you were meant to be? Who will *know* you?
When your sister is gone, her cramped room is emptied

of Bob Dylan CDs, Sunday Times pages strewn
    in all directions
like the wilderness of her thoughts longing for escape
from a mind besieged by terrors. Her tenderness trapped
    inside a dwelling

that could never be a home. Yet a life shone there, a life
    that held meaning;
in the garden of disarray a spirit still blossomed.
When your sister is gone, who will you send
    valentine roses to,

who really deserves them, and needs them
but then gives them away to someone who
   needs them more?
Who will ask if her roommate is OK, *are you OK* and
   is the world OK

even as Covid takes her from that world?
When your sister is gone, there is no poetry to read to her
that releases a vanquished body of its burden

like entering together a hushed meadow at twilight.
She knew that when a bird passes overhead
you might see only its shadow, but sometimes
   that is enough.

And because poetry is what she lived for, what made
   her heart soar—
you will write a poem, even though you both know
that you don't want *this* poem to have an ending.

Jodie Appell

Mostly I Hear Them in the Kitchen

Voices whisper they'll be here
for dinner. No need
for chairs, but please
wear the gold earrings and silk blouse,
they're so becoming.

But who will see me in them?
I won't set foot in the closet
Hangers swing like metronomes,
like empty shoulders.

As I polish candlesticks
and set out dishes,
Shut the fridge! You'll put out an eye!
Was this from childhood,
mother warning of sharp
cabinet doors?

Now that she's gone,
the stories I back into
have chipped corners.

Cathleen Cohen

Seven Candles

Tomorrow is a different kind of birthday
the seventh one so far away from me
it's not for celebrating with a party
nor wond'ring what new gift you want to see;

No, with this birth you left this earth
on your journey
you both slept and you awakened with one sigh
your essence fading faster than a mem'ry,
that which made you special turned and waved goodbye.

If you hadn't planned on staying, why'd you bother
with the living, and the leaving, in such haste?
There's a woman in the grave who lies
beside you
and I'm the one who lives on in her place--

So, tomorrow is your other, different birthday
the seventh one so far away from me
Tho' the years have brought me peace, still I remember
when you slept
and leapt into eternity.

Rose Drew

Instructions for Letting Go

She assures me
there are no rules to follow.
Just know, you don't have to let go
before you're ready
or know how you'll get to the other side,
or even how to find the path.
Sadness and tears will find you without a map or GPS.
Let them.
Grief becomes your shadow,
leads you slowly,
And although others may be on the journey with you,
You'll feel alone.

There is no need to be alarmed if tears and laughter
        take turns
as confusion and forgetting and remembering
toss and turn, unconsolable.
Thankfully, there is slumber and dreaming.
When morning comes, you
may not want to get up,
may not have what it takes to face the day.
Is it day?

Preoccupation with who is lost,
With memory,
Realizing you will never again
Sit on the bench together under the red maple
Talking and laughing
Smelling the new spring air—

In life,
we all fall prey to it—
the assumption that time goes on and on,
that there is always another chance,
another day.

This morning I had the strangest thought—
that you lost your body—
and I haven't been able to get it out of my mind.
If you were here
we would sit close and you'd cock your head to the
    side
in that way, listening, considering.
But you're not here.
I miss you.

I. Sandz

Your Grief for What You've Lost

Your grief for what you've lost lifts a mirror
up to where you're bravely working.
~ Rumi, translated by Coleman Barks

What did you think would happen
when you let go, or more accurately,
when your grip failed and the weight
of studying your pain slipped beyond
your ruminations, schematics, and chants?

Your grief for what you've lost
lifts a mirror, then drops it,
the broken shards falling slowly
until they turn into small white butterflies
disappearing like notes you never read.

Now is the time to soften your gaze
as you look out the night window
hungry for the light within.

A tree frog clings from the outside,
all of our hummingbird heart valves
opening, closing, into contours of the dark.

The sea of air that holds it all stills
to glass, then whips trees to the ground
and holds them there until the light
pulls them back up, trunks swayed,
but still honorable, each one its own
grief and its own answer to grief.

Caryn Mirriam-Goldberg

The Vigil

Tonight I sit
Alone
Keeping a vigil

Once
We shared this vigil
Then, as now, a vigil for you

Then I stayed
Not wanting you to be lonely or afraid
They'd given you a death sentence that night
How could you not be, how could I help
Hope you said was the toy bear's name, whispering
But it's too late now.

I stayed
Sitting quietly in the shadowy corner
Witnessing your goodbyes
Not knowing it was mine as well.

Now I sit
Lonely and afraid
Trying to make the best of my life
Wishing you were here, wishing I could talk with you.
Hope beside me, watching over me

You sit
Silently in the shadows where I can't
See you or hear you or touch you.

Mara Teitel Sheade

It's Time

I'm ready now for your return.
Will you come and warm a single room with your voice?
I half expect to find you cooking in the kitchen,
Your laughter filling my bed with light.

In moments I stop, listening while my heart plunges
Into the silence.
Oh, how I wish that I could sleep.
Yet waking leaves me once again alone.

I've passed the test—
I've handled papers, phone calls, letters.
And now, would that I could rest my head upon
    your shoulder
Or for a brief moment, be surprised by your smile.

Annie Brook

Once with Me

You are gone from the Earth
but never from my heart.
Who remembers, less cares
that once you were with me?

Young and fit, try again,
a girl within the year.
Three boys then follow soon,
what more could I desire?

Ten years of wear have passed.
Not so young, nor so fit
to be a mother now.
I have not forgotten;
your soul still lives with me,
a secret of my own.

Sharon R. Micenko

Nothing Like the Sun

*"Can there be friendship? I cannot see it, Will. It is a painted
statue of the Madonna, moving, but unmoved. And so, if you
are my friend, Will, it is a remarkable thing."*

—Doug Christensen, (1958-1988)

A freezing pall descends upon this house;
the leading edge arrives.
Knees to chin, recoiling from the cold smack
of sleet against the windows,
visited by spectred truths that will be owned.

Motions, moonlight, dawnings,
Sumptuous spreads of thought and sight,
and journeys into far unknowns
without each other.

Reading once again your lines upon a thin and
    common page,
the feathers of your flight
uncommon
tracings of your energies.

Trinkets, somethings, nothings,
red salt from deep within the earth,
and what words with which to fill your absence now?

No treasured packet, ribbon bound
to grace some quiet keepsake resting place,
collecting gentle fingerings along the years.

Watching as they lowered you into the earth,
Shell
within a shell,
The scrim, a lacy whispering of snow,
An eager life cried out within the womb,
and sweetly tangible, inspired release—

The lesser light to rule the night.

Carla Halversen Eskelsen

Death, 1991

My father died in September,
a week after his birthday,
eighty-five,
a doctor afraid of death,
keeping score, almost to the end,
on who showed him love and who did not.
At the end, holding my hand,
anxious to get up and leave the hospital bed.
"You're killing me."
"Come on! Let's go!"

My son killed himself in September,
a drop-out, returned to school,
trying to start over and afraid, ashamed,
a 26 year-old confidence man who conned himself
    to death.
"I want to come home and be a baby."

In October my mother was diagnosed with lung cancer.
She is 89, too old and weak for surgery or chemotherapy.
Three times a week X-rays will break her chromosomes,
    destroying
the ability of cells to divide and grow, divide and grow.
"I'm in charge here."

I am fifty-six,
still turning a compost pile,
still growing a tree.

George Hersh

What They Want to Hear

People say I'm handling it well,
  coping...
  adjusting...
But they don't know I go to sleep every night
  hugging a pillow
  pretending it's you
  and praying not to wake up
  to another morning alone.

People want to know how I'm doing
  making a new life...
  going on...
And I give a sad smile and say,
  "It's rough."
  "Thanks for asking."
  "I'm managing."
Words they want to hear.
People comment how strong and brave I've been
  through it all...
  your cancer, your fight for life, your death...
But they can't understand that
  my strength
  and bravery
  and hopes
  were buried
      with you...

Paula Porter

Going Through Her Clothes

The cashmere sweaters are flecked with tiny orange dots, as if every day was cafeteria Thursday, tomato soup and grilled cheese. Pullovers and jackets, custom-made silk outfits, some with appliqué, cardigans with Chinese coin buttons, one-of-a kind vests from the annual craft show. My mother's clothes, most of which I have never seen before, all put away for the summer, all put away dirty.

A few months after the funeral, my dad asked me to go through them. I start with a rung-out wash cloth, sponging the crusty bits off a cashmere sweater. After finishing the sixth one, I see a pattern: the right side always has the stains. No way she could reach up with a napkin, her arm paralyzed.

I take five piles of the dirtiest things to the dry cleaners, run loads in the washer, sew on loose buttons, press and fold. I do each task slowly, savoring the motions, even for clothes I know will be given away.

With each flake of crud I rub out, years of anger and frustration begin to surface. I want to find a way to erase the decades of sorrow and brokenness we shared—there was so much—and let the grief begin. I work for days on her clothes, feeling the full force of my anger and despair.

I decide to pack away some of her nicest sweaters in tissue paper, box and seal them up like a wedding dress. I look for tissue paper, but I don't have any except the kind with Christmas trees. I want to preserve the clothes: I can't preserve the visits.

I think of a documentary I saw about Hindu funeral ceremonies. The female relatives wash the dead woman's body, anoint it with ghee, dress her in clean white linen before her son places her on the funeral pyre. As I continue to clean, a truth comes to light like the tarnished silver mirror I just polished, the one I found in the bottom of her pocketbook.

I am doing something more than working on my mother's clothes. I must be making a kind of offering, performing a sacrament or a penance of my own design.

It's like I'm washing my mother's body.

At the same time, I understand what compelled faithful people to save a dead man's things: a tooth, a hem of a garment, a piece of the arrow that killed him, a drop or two of his blood, put them in jeweled reliquaries. But you can only save what you can see or touch. As if I am outside the scene, I watch myself lift a sleeve of beige angora to my lips and inhale the scent of her one last time.

Jill Jennings

Secret Message

I hear you in my voice,
now that yours is stilled forever.
I hear you in my voice:
an inflection or choice of words,
shrugging my shoulders in that certain way;
now a secret message between us.
It's all I have left of you.

Mike Bernhardt

Today is My 38th Birthday...

Today is my 38th birthday, the first without Richie
no flowers will be sent no phone call no card
just the memory of other birthdays and his love for me
tucked
away
inside my heart.

Suzanne Fried-Freed

The Promise

Let me necklace together
  a string of memory moments,
  lingering on one
  that glistens most:

We stand under the
  wedding canopy
  while the rabbi's
  blessings embrace us.

A bead of sweat
  irreligiously drops down
  his face to poise
  like a remembered prayer.

The solemn quiet is
  splintered by the glass
  smashed under my beloved's heel
  and I see my
  dead mother again
  in the sun-darkening room.

She spreads the canopy's
   fringe-fingers
   for the sunsetting ray
   to bless us with a
   promise...
   even in its dying.

My beloved too, promised
   to keep the canopy
   hovering forever,
   but only an etched promised
   "forever"
   on the wedding band
   remains.

I squeeze the shining moments
   like prayer beads
   tightly in my
   widowed
   wedding-banded hand.

Pauline K. Schmookler

Letter to Adam

Dear Adam,

It means so much to me to have you to talk with. Knowing that you love and miss your brother as I love and miss Paul makes me feel less alone.

I don't feel like I have a family anymore. It's like we're now just two parents and a kid. I hate it when people ask me if I have any brothers or sisters. I don't know whether to say, "Yes, but he died," or "No," and then get the old, "Oh, you're a spoiled only child." Why do people say that?

It's weird now, because when I'm mad at Mommy or Daddy I can't go to Paul and complain and feel supported, but when they're mad at me they can still go to each other. In fact, they support each other in dealing with Paul's death and I wish I had Paul to support me through this. Now, if I go to, say, my dad because I'm sad, my mom feels left out so I'm really alone.

I've been holding off on this question but I really need to know: How should I act with my parents when they're upset about losing their only son and they become too overprotective and restrictive? I try to be extra good so they'll not have to worry about me and they'll not miss Paul so much, but it's a big job trying to fill the void. My parents try to be there for me but...I don't know.

I wish I still saw life like other kids my age...shopping, parties, dates, sports, etc. I feel too wise for my age. I don't want to be like this. I've felt a lot of pain, as though my heart actually broke in two—cracked, shattered into so many pieces that it could never be reassembled. Will I ever get over this loneliness? Will I ever have someone in my life again with whom I can be as close as Paul and I were? If I do will they leave too? Do you wonder about these things too, Adam?

Love,

Kathleen

Kathleen M. Johansen
(Written at age 18)

Calling Me Meg

I could choose a harp-full heaven.
Choirs and flights of angels.
Exultation.
Peace.
Freedom from pain.
Everlasting joy.
Coming home to a compassionate God.
That heaven, I could predict
and would quickly find lacking.

The heaven I hope for,
would last only a moment
and be held in a single word,
in hearing your voice
calling me "Meg".

Maggie Jackson

Offerings

Black tear in the earth,
reflects his image
through the names.
He caresses a name engraved
into the ebony chevron,
memorizing it with his fingertips.
Then rubs a stubby, yellow pencil
against a torn piece of white paper
held against panel 27E,
holding his son's name to heart.

Paula Porter

The Garden of Dreams

Some dreams are nothing more than dreams. Others are like... visitations. There is no symbolism or metaphor. These dreams are so real that we know without a doubt that our loved one is letting us know that they are safe. These dreams are immediate, powerful and memorable. Often, we learn something about love, life, death and the survival of Spirit. Whether we awaken joyous or miserable, these dreams almost always help us to heal.

Conversations

In my dream last night
You weren't dead...
You lived,
But I said, "No, you can't be here,
              You're still dead."
I argued with you.
    "I've changed.
    "Your dying made me different.
    "Everything would change again.
    "I love you, but you're dead.
    "You can't come back."

And you said,
    "I was only checking.
    "I love you.
    "Don't forget me...
    "Please"

How can I?

Paula Porter

Resurrection

"How could you be here?"
"I don't know," you answered.
But we smiled and embraced
love washing through us
as I closed my eyes to listen
and you spoke to me of dying

"I remember it was eleven o'clock.
They were wheeling me out of the room.
Then I was trying to get back,
running through the corridors,
but I couldn't find the room.
I didn't realize..."

you recalled it with a sense of wonder
no pain, no fear—a magical adventure
and as you spoke:
an all-encompassing quiet joy
your heart smiling
my heart opening

but I awoke, too soon
feeling you in my arms
as you evaporated.
I laughed, then cried
your words echoing in my ears
so loudly I still hear them.

Mike Bernhardt

Reunion

Strolling in a river, I meet You.
Catching the eager rush of my
affection at arm's length, You hold
my eyes long with yours, before
embracing. I feel your thinness,
the lesions on your back (places
where they'd never really been).

We walk together arm in arm
as so many times before, and
head uphill toward the lodge until
I say I ought to find the car.
You think it can wait, but I
nonetheless walk off to search.

Only then, it comes to me:
How could I have left You?
And turning, I see all has changed.
The path is empty and I'm alone
with only the memory of
You in my arms.

I know the river has nourished
three seasons since You last walked
into my arms; and I can feel
how precious it has been
to hold You
Once
Again.

Carlin Paige Holden

Three Days After Allen Died

Before you sat on the edge of my bed,
I could feel you in the air around me
like Ophelia's shawl floating downstream,
more than a ghost haunting:
it was truly you.

Light concentrated like pinspots
on three tracks picking out your aura
water-lily-like
peaking at your seven chakras:
the light opened and you stepped through.

A tree squirrel clawed
the shake roof over your head.
Your hand warmed as you curled the light
into small orbs between your palms,
brushed its heat against my cheek.

In your eyes words sparkled
like shooting stars,
sounds pressed onto my lips, alternating
crimson and turquoise, visual sentences
about the cosmic dust of your journey.

From the tips of both hands you threw
the orbs off. I could hear your voice:
    "Everything I had feared is not here.
    I don't know yet what is;
    but I know I do not fear."

Long silence engulfed us as we sat,
not touching, as if you were me.
The floorboards hummed an ancient elegy;
my eyes closed in harmony. In sleep,
I could feel you still.

Sam Ambler

To Papa Whom I Don't Remember

I talked to you once
   in a dream
   when Alice-like
   I slithered into a hole
   and looked for you.

You came
   skeletal frame undulating
   skinless mouth ululating
   sounds I translated and
   shaped into ideas never
   shared between us since
   I had no language
   when you died.

In the dream's darkness
   I can't remember what we said
   or what language we spoke,
   but un-babel like
   I understood you
   and you me,
   just as you had, I'm sure,
   my baby babblings.

It was enough that we talked
for I was no longer alone,
and I could climb out of my dream
knowing, Papa, that
there is a link now,
a line,

A continuum.

Pauline K. Schmookler

Begin to Heal

Slowly, we find that we are stronger as the storm blows through us. Stronger, but more like bamboo than oak—we find that we can bend more before we break. In the pain we begin to find the seeds of healing and rebirth. We discover new meaning in old pieces of our lives and create new pieces to replace those that have lost their meaning. We find pleasure in giving away a possession of our loved one's to someone who will treasure it. We visit places that our loved one enjoyed and find comfort that softens and sweetens our grief.

little words

sun fades in streaks across the rosewood panels
tap tap, others join our stiffened shadows
rustling, choosing, settling
a collective deep breath
braced and waiting
finally
the little words begin
    small and hobbling
    bent whisperings so needed
    tiny peeps between our aching hearts
    they stretch and try, then lift to their reluctant flight
    laden with dark gifts and tinsel twine
        now perched and softly warbling
        accompany a sigh, a sob
        well, I do remember when he...
        oh, yes, I know too, and I, how can it be...
        eyes glaze into what was
            come little words
            coo and nest on my right shoulder
            for death has claimed the left
            brush your feathery strokes upon my soul
            preening in compassion's pool

Dixie Pine

The Journey

There is a place in me where you live
A wide-eyed wondering place
    of smells and touches and discovery
We were co-explorers, you and I
Dancing the dance of learning
Together

Alone
My healing comes slowly
My new learning the dance of death
Your death.
Again, I am wide-eyed and wondering
My discovery the depth of your love
And mine.

Beyond the known I dance
From the depths of my pain
I surrender
With an aching heart
I open
It is all that I can do.

Annie Brook

Source
(for Tammy)

When all becomes quiet and still
I find myself looking for the person I used to be.
When endings become beginnings and
The hours seem to have dissolved into
Nothing
I find myself wondering
Where have I been?
When the stars take over
Or a sliver of moon crescents the darkened sky,
Eyes adjusting to the newfound light,
I find myself staring into the obscurity of the past.
When everything around me screams to *awake,*
    awake, awake and sing!
I find myself persisting that I am lost and can never be
    found.
When all that seemed to matter is gone
And sandcastles are rebuilt out of air
When the eagle lands,
Without grace,
When the dragonfly
Silently drowns,
When the whale shores up,
Too tired,
To swim,
And spouts a final tornado,
I momentarily know:
finding myself was never the point at all.

Dorothy Lemoult

So I Will Light a Candle

For him
For the frightened, angry
Boy who lived inside
For the confused
And fearsome man
Who raged against the world
And railed against
His life
For the running man
Whose demons finally
Overtook him
I will light a candle and say
Be at peace
Be at peace now.
Even while I know that
Peace is the other thing
Beside his life
that he took from me

Nori J. Rost

Years of Tears

When they came, they were unstoppable.
Years and years and years of tears poured forth
Silently screaming out of their pain.

Tears unknown, unrecognizable, hidden
    behind a fear so profound.
Ah, but she knew, that little girl who cried,
    "Daddy, daddy, where are you? I want you!"

Emptiness now, tired.
Peace eludes me still.
Searching for the slender thread that I hope
    still binds me to my dad.

It is there, I know it, deep inside me.
Shining filament, strong as a spider's web.
Broken now, but waiting, waiting…

Renee Esposito

To Heal

Grief
deeply embedded in a soul
can twist and turn
can swell and strew poison.

Let it go, you say
move on, you say
vent the tears and anger
move on, you say.

Yell at God
Yell at you for leaving me
move on, you say

Look again into the sky
and see the clouds
smell the rain
touch another human in
a loving manner

begin to heal.

Monica Jean Davis

A Sister's Response

I didn't know
about so many moments.
You were nearly
ten years young
when I was born.
Ten years of
distance and time.

Your lost children.
I knew of one,
but not of the many.

I knew of your pain,
the grief, anger, fierceness.
But, from what origins, depths
I didn't know.

You wrote of the moment
of finding our mother.
You, not quite 16,
I, a mere 6.

I remember your screams
as I played with neighbor kids,
Tommy and Karen
across the street.
Their mother rushed out,
relieved that we were OK.

Neighbors, next door and beyond
came running
to help, to comfort,
stoically hiding their
shock and sorrow.

Calls to my father,
police, fire department,
gently guided us to our backyard
as they completed
their grim work.

So much in-between
I don't remember
until our mother was laid to rest,
a foreshadowing of
her forever absence.

I didn't know.
Rest in peace, dear sister.

Debra Ann Halloran

Facing Fears

I fear somehow I might forget
your lovely eyes and face, and yet
I know that this will never be.
But nonetheless, it bothers me.

I fear to smile if good days come:
but glad I'm here, no longer numb,
afraid that joy could maybe mean
I'm past it now, not in-between.

I fear the days of tears and pain
and hurting that will come again
to strike me hard with waves of grief,
to test my strength and my belief.

I fear the loss of memories
and now, it brings me to my knees.
I fear these things but I'll survive.
My love for you keeps me alive.

Ken Slesarik

There is a Love Born of Tears

There is a love born of tears
and a love born from tears,
a crack of hope born from this weeping.

I breathe deep and long
in an attempt to come home to myself,
and I breathe empty and full
in an attempt to come home to you,

I sing daily songs of sacrifice
and see the small joy of a daffodil
reaching into its blooming from under ice.

Some days there is only this reminder,
and my startled answer to your unvoiced words,
some days there is only this moment
followed by the next one,

as I remember that I do not know,
that I have not yet stood out in the rain today,
and have not yet spoken to God,

that I have come this long way to reach you,
to learn that love carries sorrow within it.

Lucy Trevitt

God Shuts the Door
and Opens a Window

My heart has led me to this place,
  where now I see you in
  other women's heartful acts.

Where courage is born of love,
  is where I see you clearest.

Then, I cry because I know
  I've lost you.

Then, I cry because I know
  I've found you again.

You're gone,
  and you're everywhere.

In your going,
  I've found your essence.

Anonymous

Discovery

Through the agony of grief
   I found reverence for life.
Through the long, lonely nights
   When all I wanted was his arms around me,
   I found joy in giving love freely.
Through my tears and sorrow,
   I found friends to help bear my burdens.
Through his death
   I found myself.

Paula Porter

Letter to Daniel Sheridan Fulkerson (1942-1972)

Father,
Miles Davis makes love to his
   trumpet and makes it live as
I stare at the map in front of
me
   your address whispers to me
      section 23
      lot 35
      grave 16
In West gate main entrance off
   Mormon Bridge Road past
office left at 27 Faith
   past 27 Memories and 27
C.C. past 29 Meditation and
29 New Memorial and 29 Old Memorial
   large curving triangle marked with 23
in black on this folded and crumpled
map to you
      entrance open daily 8 a.m.

      why can i not bring myself to visit you?
i never have except for
   once when i was younger but
that doesn't count because I don't
remember it except for the triangle
   you left when i was one
so i don't even have any memories

of you to hold on to
just a class ring from 1960 that
    I wear every day
and some View-Master reels which
    i've never looked at
    and an October 17, 1959
Omaha World Herald with the headline
"North's Power Shades Prep's Passing in
    20-19 Display of Offensive Might"
for no apparent reason
    some mechanical drawing awards
from your senior year and your
    army jacket and watch and
some cufflinks

    all meaningless but I hold
onto them in the hope that someday
maybe i'll understand the man in
    the pictures holding a newborn
baby boy

    hoping that maybe someday i'll
understand why you committed
suicide
in our garage with the
    car running and the door down

(continued)

149

perhaps someday i'll understand God
        enough to thank Him that Mom
and i made it through the night at
    the hospital almost dying of
carbon monoxide poisoning ourselves

    I long to have known you
but instead have an emptiness in
    my Self that's numb from the
        years of never really
comprehending who you were and
    finally realizing that i never
        would

These trinkets will teach
    me nothing but i will
hold on to them Father
    out of respect for the
type of man i've been told you
were
because you were my father
    if not by blood then by
love

the stuffed Snoopy in the
pictures has been loved to threads
   and he now rests in a drawer
under my bed
   and sometimes i
think that maybe you put a little of your
   love into that stuffed animal
      and that i reaped the
benefits of that love for years

      I'll visit you Father—when
i'm ready to put the make
   believe behind and face the cold
stone home of your residence—
      because i love you
         Just give me time,

         Son

Robert Fulkerson

151

I Said Goodbye to Ghosts Today

I said goodbye to ghosts today...
   ghosts of men I never really knew,
   but their names will be on my heart forever.
Men whom I never met, who never met me,
   and whose lives are joined with mine for eternity.
Ten names, written on the stone of my heart,
names which will never appear on this black granite.
Names known only to a few, fates known only to their
   God...
I know their names.

Tim Cannon

Buds at the End of Winter

My grief lives on in me,
an old moldy stump
rotting soft in the woods.
Or a tree in late winter,
buds appearing
red and green on bare branches.

Mike Bernhardt

My Mother Rises

In shafts of morning light pollen rises from the duff.
We four sisters linger over the skeleton of a baby crow
its delicate beak agape, ribs scattered
like eyelashes. I kneel to cover the remains

with fragrant balsam branches, my heart cleaving.
We, the living, go on, hoping for a gentle afterlife.
But you, mother, are no more than fine grit in the bottom
of the bowl we carry. Is hope the same as prayer?

Ghost pipes haunt the undergrowth with eerie music.
Sunlight paints leaves like scattered heartbeats.
There is no gravesite. We follow your wishes.
Your ashes dust fern fronds and wintergreen.

A bird whistle pierces languid air. We raise our quiet
faces to the trill. How strange it is that you are not with us.
You would know the warbler's name and answer it's call.
The bird vanishes into the canopy, the way you rise.

When our walk is over, we will head to our separate
homes. I will peel apples, slice them and powder them
with cinnamon and sugar. One of us will knead bread.
Later we will sleep in our restless beds.

I imagine your suffering is over. What if I could once more
feel your soft hand in mine? We would sit side by side
at the end of the dock, trail our bare feet in cool
lake water and watch stars ignite one after another.

Dale Champlin

Andalucian Wood

the bits and pieces of paper i have gathered
paper that holds memory for me
holy cards imprinted with prayers to alleviate sorrow,
newspaper clippings in odd shapes skirt the inner
    landscape of my box of
Andalucian wood
long i have held memory here
long since the time of my recovery has this box
    embraced the forms of
events that have occurred in this my new life
i wonder
do we hold onto the spirits of those we have loved,
    those we knew
i wonder,
do we bind them to earth by refusing to let them go?
or is it a quality of being human that keeps us grasping at
    bits of paper, at
validation of memories and arms that no longer hold us in
    the moment's
dance
i wonder
do we trust ourselves so little that we hang on so tightly?
as if anyone really could erase the embers of our soul.

Catherine Firpo

Pebbles of Sorrow

When the day had dawned,
you, who, I thought would
outlast stormy winds like Albatross
left for the other side.
You took your interrupted dreams with you,
while your wide eyes were begging God
to let you stay with your loved ones,
with your flower garden that you adored so much
and the moonlight
that you slept under with open eyes.
But ruthless death sneaked upon you
and snapped your breath.

Your kind voice has stretched
into the maze of my memory.
I walk in front of the moon and behind the moon
carrying with both hands a heavy pain,
which in vain I try to let go.
I wish I had watered your flower garden as often
    as you wanted.
Pebbles of grief block my breathing passage
I have wept all my tears and have undergone
    all my regrets.
I feel trapped in sorrow like bait in a spider's web.
But, you return in my dreams with forgiving eyes
and somehow lighten the weight on my shoulders.

Fereshteh Sholevar

UnBirthday

I wished for peace, I have it now:
a gentle giving back of you;
hard-won peace: so betrayed by fate, by life, by you—

So many times this day is just a secret:
when women talk of birth,
compare notes and battle scars,
Me too! I want to shout, me too, I have advice
on first versus second birth,
on drugs—pros and cons, on how
no two pregnancies are the same,
nor labour, nor child;
ask me, I know.

I wait and wait, past years, past decades,
past even grief and still I cannot let your life
fall carelessly from my lips,
revealing all I know. Not pity
do I want or need, just you:
the realness of you,
our adventures of birth and bath,
smiles and howls,
first-time moments bittersweet,
but sweet all the same;
my birth too.

I love how you've changed me,
forced courage from me, empathy, anger,
passions I had left behind or maybe never had, gifts.
What expensive gifts, this heart that breaks,
these eyes that weep,
my wild urge to shield children in my arms,
soothe and listen,
remind them they are love made life,
a hundred years of promise, I love this—

—and what I take from this day is strength,
hope, finality,
a tiny moment of furious loss
a glance at your rare photograph, and then just
        another day—

I wished for peace, I have it now,
a gentle giving back of you,
no beaten breast, no rent clothing:
an unbirthday of the most unsplendid kind.

Rose Drew

Things I Can't Believe

I can't believe that life is short
or that water isn't blue,
it just reflects the blue sky.

And I can't believe that there's life that I do not know of.
Or that the world is round.
And the earth is millions of years old.

Most of all I can't believe that when people die
    they're gone.
Because I know they aren't.
They're just hidden in my heart.

Robin Lahargoue Shorett
(Written at age 12)

In the Bookstore

Wandering in the bookstore
trying hoping to catch her eye,
Ted Hughes under my arm.
Will she notice I'm a poet?

Watching the faces I read
poetry in the corner.
A face I know!
but hide from.

I read creation myths,
creating my own.
I have been to hell
and back

and begin again
to hope
lost
in a bookstore.

Mike Bernhardt

I Have Begun Writing

Words springing up from the
    newly tilled and sown field
of this bitter earth;

an explosion
    of dark blossoms.

I try to pick a few,
    lush with barely ripened grief,
to press
between the brittle
pages
    of this new reality,
to preserve forever
their terrible beauty.

But now I have to leave;
I have an appointment
and I am going to be late
as it is.

Frantically I grab a pencil and an old envelope;
I want to write down these ideas
before I leave—
as if I couldn't remember them,
as if they weren't forever a part of
the landscape of my soul—
I want to be sure these thoughts aren't lost
to the busy-ness of
    "life goes on"
So I jot them down:
    The family
    The phone call
    The shot to the heart

Nori J. Rost

The Breath of Great Spirit

There will never be a time when we have completely gotten over and forgotten our loss. But we can find a place for it. As we rebuild our lives, we learn to let go of all that will never be. We may discover in the process, however, that it is only our old ways of living to which we must say goodbye, not our loved ones—they continue to live in our hearts. It is then that we may be able to find a gift in our loss: we have become more for losing what was precious to us.

I Thought of You Today

I thought of you today.
I watched hawk dive out of the sky
and crash upon its prey
as I sat next to you—
at least I thought it was you—I couldn't be sure
there is no marker yet to name the spot where you lay.
So I ran my hands along grass
finding the crumpled earth from the spot where
    they had dug—
finding the line of the piece of land which now
    covers you,
you, my beloved Father—
and the grief hits upon my head as the light from the sun
sending cold silver tears
splashing off my face into the wind.
The wind, all I ever hear up here is the wind!
Doesn't it ever stop blowing up here?
No wonder hawk hovers so long in the ice blue sky
the breath of the great spirit is strong here
it is a good sweet place for your body to lay.
I miss your body, I miss the smell of you Father—
I miss your arms around me in a hug, and I miss the
resonance of your voice.

I thought of you today.
I watched hawk hover low,
cloud shadow embrace mountain,
blue of ocean touch sky,
sweet brown green of earth
warmed by sun.
I thought of you today,
I rose with imprint of grass on my legs,
the hum of tears in my head
and the silent sound of your voice
filling my heart
and the breath of great spirit kissing my face.
I thought of you today.

Catherine Firpo

Around the Block

Mornings much cooler on hot Texas summer days
but 7:00 pm was your choice to take a walk
daily timing yourself from-to the front door
re-entering with declaration of minutes: 7 your best

Neighbors were startled, knowing your diagnosis,
and I confess those were long minutes for me
sitting with fingers laced inside that front door
trusting Spirit to buoy your energies, guide your feet

Now you are free-walking over the rainbow bridge
perhaps taking giant leaps cloud-to-cloud
like your youthful leaps on the backyard trampoline
before responsibilities, future still uncharted

I anchor in the chair opposite yours, now empty,
marveling—that you came into my life,
that you departed your body with relative ease,
amid family blessed by your 46 years

And last night at 7:00 I rose from this chair
to walk around the block, each step tracing yours,
guided and buoyed by the sense of you watching

I'll walk with you again tonight

Jazz Jaeschke Kendrick

Christopher

We wanted you,
looked forward to meeting you,
To discovering who you are;
Your selfness.

With excitement, anticipation,
Love and joy
We waited,
Your arrival.

Your reasons for not staying
Are your own.

Your earthly family loves you.
We send you
OUR PEACE.

Talitha Anne Hostetter

Alan

in my memory
yesterday is today
and you are here
we talk in the garden
of dreams
you live your yesterdays
forever 35
i live my todays
growing older
but you gained wisdom in death
forbidden in your life
i turn to you for answers
refuge from my fears
like you protected me
when i was a little girl
my big brother
to whom i brought teddy bears

whose fear cut through my heart
to the tenderness in my soul
till i became your protector
staying with you through hospital nights
wiping your brow, getting lemon candies,
holding your hand
wishing you well on a journey
i couldn't comprehend
but only hope is better
than where you came from
where your todays are endless
moments flying free,
your spirit the light
you ached for it to be
and your yesterdays float
into tomorrow

Mara Teitel Sheade

centerpart

eyes open,
eyes closed,
in silence,
in a storm,
you are everywhere.

next to me
you caress
my thoughts,
becoming
part of my center,
my strength.

i want to hold you
but
you are everywhere,
unbound by form,
accessible but unreachable.

with vigor
and excitement
about to burst,

i run home hoping
to capture
your playful smile,
until
standing alone,
i realize
you have departed

you've become
part of my center,
part of everything
i feel and touch.

blossoming
in the puddles
the thunderous storm
has left,
you whisper hello,
reminding me
to close my eyes
and whisper
"goodbye."

Jill Iris Bacharach

Holly's Life and Death Were
Made of Panache

In the final moment of Edmond Rostand's play Cyrano de Bergerac,
Cyrano, declares he has one thing left without spot
or wrinkle that he can call his own. . .

Et, c'est. . .mon panache
-Cyrano de Bergerac

What now?!
-Holly Fox

Your last action
in this life
was to fling
your breath out
the very last one
singular and
specific, a whole
lifetime felt
in what you flung
forward, this invisible
inspiration
skipped hard
& struck the moment's
surface, then gone
and done, to disappear
into depthlessness.

And immediately
I thought of
the way you kicked
your sneakers off
with a deliberate
panache, that was
uniquely your own
in a gesture of
delight, confident
in your powers
to give flight, a carefree
challenge to gravity's
grave utility,
making sure your day
came to a close
with joy unfettered.

John Fox

174

Eileen

Our acquaintance seemingly brief
inside a timeless sacred space,
I will remember you.
I will remember your hand
resting gracefully on a pillow,
beautiful long fingers with manicured nails
peach colored, like your blanket.
I will remember your eyes meeting mine
as we sat together in the silence.
I will remember you allowing me to
touch and warm the body
you were soon to leave.
I will remember you making the effort to speak
to tell me the massage felt good
and to thank me for coming.
Yet it is I who must thank you
for your gift of sharing
with me, a fellow traveler,
those simple truthful moments
in the journey of your life.

Dawn Nelson

Dear Mark

Dear Mark...
   Son, friend, brother,
    Student of philosophy,
     Artist, dancer, lover,
      Realist and dreamer,
       Traveler to exotic places,
        Wishing now to be a UFO...

As you prepare to fly away,
   I bow in gratitude...
You are a shining light...
   My teacher, my patient, my student,
   My absolver.
It was heaven to be forgiven—
   The blessing of a second chance bestowed.

Go, then...
   Take off in your blue and silver rocket.
   Explore the galaxies in all your splendor,
    elegant and bold.

Go in peace and safety—
You are protected by an awesome golden light.

I join everyone who loves you
    In wishing you Godspeed.
A part of us goes with you,
    A part of you remains in our hearts.

You have given us so much in your receiving of our love
Your tears have told us all we need to know...

    Heart of hearts, rose quartz,
        Pink and silver skies,
    Sea green eyes...

Dear Mark,
    Goodbye.

Frances Richey

Madagascar

In Madagascar, when trees burn,
the hot sap sings of ancient roots
buried under ashes. The trees burn
to clear land to feed cattle,
bony, lowing, head-swinging riches.
Cattle horns adorn ancestral tombs.

Aunt Rakotosamimanana will come home
for the holidays. She has been dead one year.
Auntie joins the family at the feasting,
lying in state on the sideboard,
more mute than wood.

Last spring, I planted you in the ground.
There you grow, like your roses (red as
sunset, red as flames), mute. I adorn
my rooms with roses and
often sing of you.

Penelope Kellogg Winkler

The Disclaimer

I mean no disrespect
But I think,
If the doctors had known him
The way some of us knew him

They would have made
The recipients sign
An iron clad disclaimer,

Because there was a part of him
So ingrained in his very cells
That somewhere,

Some young boy or girl
With a new life may have found
An obsession to be near an old dusty pitcher's mound
And smile a sheepish grin.

Terry Ray Van Huss

Yahrzeit

WAX in a glass.
The wick is lit
   and congealed memories melt
   into a liquid pool
   like old tears once shed.

Now the flame is warm
   companionable
   comforting
   like a presence.

Through the window
   I see the changing leaves
   on Yahrzeit oaks
   announcing their yearly death
   in flame leaf-tongues.

That was their dirge in other years.
Today the fiery leaves are
   exuberant in their
   exaltation of this color moment.

"Now" the leaf says
"Now" the answering flame flickers.

Through the window
   they whisper to each other
   and in the Yahrzeit glass
   warm memories float peacefully
   in watery wax.

Pauline K. Schmookler

Canary Bird Zinnias

In the days before you died,
in the increasing swelter of August,
I could wait no longer: the bare spots
between greenery cried out for
whatever bits of color the depleted
nurseries might have.

Five months in, we are all depleted,
so I migrated, masked, to the place
of baby plants, commandeered a cart
without wondering if it had been wiped
clean, then lingered under the misters,
surprised by the bounty, fingering leaves
of the still-green.

I'd read the word "hospice" in the email
from your youngest daughter, allowed it
to hover around the perimeter of my body
but go no further.

Looking for perennials—they last longer—
I selected small plastic pots, late bloomers
sending up shoots of color, looking for buds
that might decide to show themselves
in the coming weeks. I skipped the annuals—
gone too soon—except for the fluffy yellow
canary zinnias, tall and perky on strong

(continued)

stems, smiling at me, moving my hand
to pat one, pulling it into my cart.

Several times a day, I'd close my eyes,
wish you love on your journey,
imagine you in that liminal space,
the final discoveries of a lifetime,
prayerful lines of poetry running
behind your closed eyes.

I brought the plants home, watered them,
let them sit on the deck for a couple of days
before I sank to my knees on the foam kneeler,
my form of prayer, hands in dirt, never gloved,
usually accumulating nicks and gouges
along the way. Digging first, estimating the
depth needed to receive the newcomer, trying
to remove it from its plastic skin without
yanking, fluffing the tendrils of roots
before tenderly setting it into the hole.

Once, when I visited, we planted annuals
outside your house, under the living room
windows, the old siding a softer yellow than

canary yellow zinnias. Your hands ungloved,
veins pulsing with purpose, me handing
over a trowel like a surgical assistant,
you smiling, happy in the work.

This week in my backyard I wasn't planting you.
Others would do that two days after your liftoff
into mystery. I didn't think in metaphor, so busy
was I tending the living. It's only now—
hand watering the buoyant flowers, some heads
browning, new ones on their way to blossom—
that I notice the optimistic heads of volunteer
yellow zinnias in the round clay bowl on the deck,
years after their ancestors grew there.

I see that you were planting me, as you did
thousands of times—with plants, with poems,
with people—gently setting us into place,
unaware of your hands patting the earth
around our growing stems, our roots belled into
a delicate skirt comingling with worms,
diving deeply into the dark.

Jan Haag

The Argument against Letting Go

My mother still
won't let me wear
tops with wide horizontal stripes
and she's been dead ten years.
They make me look too short
she says.

You'd think I wouldn't need
to listen to her any more.
You're wrong.

You'd say I could
go shopping without her.
I could.
But I usually don't.

You see,
Given the choice between
joking with her in the dressing room
about the styles and the salesgirls,

Enjoying with her the beauty of
this knit, that color,
Hanging out together
in such a comfortable way
Just us two,

Given the choice between that
and the green beige pink
horizontal striped sweater
I passed up yesterday,
Given that choice,
I opted again for Mom.
Can you blame me?

Wendy Lichtman

Major Ballou's Letter

Editor's note: I first saw this letter on the PBS series, "The Civil War." It was written by Major Sullivan Ballou to his wife, about a week before he died in the first battle of Bull Run in Virginia. I was so moved by its message of eternal love that I ordered a copy to give to my wife Susan, but it finally arrived about two weeks after her death. I have included it here with the thought that it may be as meaningful to you as it still is to me.

July 14, 1861
Camp Clark, Washington

My very dear Sarah:

The indications are very strong that we shall move in a few days—perhaps tomorrow. Lest I should not be able to write again, I feel impelled to write a few lines that may fall under your eye when I shall be no more...

I have no misgivings about, or lack of confidence in, the cause in which I am engaged, and my courage does not halt or falter. I know how strongly American Civilization now leans on the triumph of the Government, and how great a debt we owe to those who went before us through the blood and sufferings of the Revolution. And I am willing—perfectly willing—to lay down all my joys in this life, to help maintain this Government, and to pay that debt...

Sarah, my love for you is deathless, it seems to bind me with mighty cables that nothing but Omnipotence could break; and yet my love of Country comes over me like a strong wind and bears me irresistibly on with all these chains to the battlefield.

The memories of the blissful moments I have spent with you come creeping over me, and I feel most gratified to God and to you that I have enjoyed them so long. And hard it is for me to give them up and burn to ashes the hopes of future years, when, God willing, we might still have lived and loved together, and seen our sons grown up to honorable manhood around us. I have, I know, but few small claims upon Divine Providence, but something whispers to me—perhaps it is the wafted prayer of my little Edgar, that I shall return to my loved ones unharmed. If I do not my dear Sarah, never forget how much I love you, and when my last breath escapes me on the battlefield, it will whisper your name. Forgive me my many faults, and the pains I have caused you. How thoughtless and foolish I have often times been! How gladly would I wash out with my tears every little spot upon your happiness

But O Sarah, if the dead can come back to this earth and flit unseen around those they have loved, I shall always be near you: in the gladdest days and in the darkest nights... always, always, and if there be a soft breeze upon your cheek, it shall be my breath, as the cool air fans your throbbing temple, it shall be my spirit passing by. Sarah, do not mourn me dead; think I am gone and wait for thee, for we shall meet again.

Pantheist

She had walked these trails, these beaches,
Caught her spirit in foliage, sand, and rock.
She had rubbed her feet in pale phosphorescence
And chased the teasing water which curled
Its tendrils in darkness cobwebbed with
Moon and stars.

She had seen dark waters dispelled
In ringing bursts of light and spray;
Had climbed the living mounds,
Reached angular granite, had touched
Shadows, cavern depth and pool shallows.
She had breathed in the great Sequoias,
Knew their texture, their beasts, their birds
As companion, had understood flight.

She had heard the resonant thunder of the blow-hole
Sound its consistent note, had bent
Into hollow spaces, emerged into openness,
Lending herself to the aweful power
Which sent its bulk against the cliffs:
Rush and the weight dissipated; rush and the rock
Creviced, weakened and split,
Divided and carried away. She took her place
In eternal passage.

Now she has rejoined herself,
Merged again, part and pattern
Of the light, the season, the day.
Shed of sensation and the smaller activity,
Shed of mortal fears, the stillness of her body
Has returned to the larger motion.

She is a part of the force
That divides the waves and whips the concealing dunes
Into concentric piles. She has returned
To the original creation—no tears, no blood,
No bones. She moves anew in the heavy living waters
And disintegrating stone, in landslide and germination,
In the winged hunter hawk and the turn
Of the earth alternating darkness
And light, in the wild grass
And the mobile arc of cliffs and shore.

Freed, she invades all the hidden places;
Her self, only consciousness lost,
Is caught into process—part of the moving heart,
Part of the wind, part of the power
And all the unchanging beauty as long
As the wild beauty endures.

Elizabeth Léonie Simpson

Time Passes

Bright red dragonfly hovers by my face,
slips off and returns again and again.
Cat watches with vague interest
from his shaded lair under the patio table.
Yvonne tends the flowers,
picks a zucchini and strawberries for dinner.
Life continues now
as if you had never been here,
though I am here because of you.

Your death connected me forever
to what lies beyond this world.
I felt that Light inside me, always;
rudderless, beguiled, I longed to join it.
But, time passes
Yvonne is smiling at me, we talk
of dreams, and having children
this garden is exploding with life
and I am no longer in any hurry to leave.

Mike Bernhardt

In Bud

So much is in bud,
Even as you fade like the long shadows
of light at evening time
burnished with golden hue.

So much is in bud, as you unfold and unfurl
moving towards a threshold
that only you can enter.

So much is in bud,
as you pass through a doorway woven
with blossoms of beginnings and endings.

And who can say which is which?

Susan O'Connell

Coo-Whit—A Read-Aloud Story

Round Robin called three times... coo-whit, coo-whit, coo-whit. Leaves rustled. Dog, splashing down by the creek, perked one ear. Yet all else was still. Coo-whit, coo-whit, coo-whit. Her voice sang out clear in the brisk blue air.

She sighed and turned away, disappointed. It had been months since she had last seen Friend. It was the night of the big storm and Friend had been blown away by Great Wind. Round Robin wondered, as she had every day since, if Friend was still alive or if her broken body lay silently hid amongst the faraway grasses.

It was the not-knowing that was the hardest. Coo-whit, coo-whit, coo... Round Robin was no longer conscious of how often she called. Robin had always thought she would know when Death reached near, as if she would hear a deep bell inside her heart. Yet she heard no bell, and felt no gray ghost creeping near. Only her heart ached with a longing that sometimes throbbed so deeply she could not hear her own song.

How was it, she wondered, that one little bird friend could mean so much and come so close? She hadn't known Friend long. It was barely past the gathering time when they met, both busy pulling worms left in the harvested fields. She laughed with the memory of Friend tugging madly at a terrifically huge worm which clung fast to the roots of the corn stalks.

Neither bird nor worm would give in to the struggle and neither one would let go. Flooding thoughts came back now of bright moon nights too beautiful to sleep through, of shared stories and lilting harmonies of song. Oh, how good to have a Friend!

Coo-whit, coo-whit, coo-whit. Round Robin rustled her feathers. Who was this death? Had death taken Friend away with the wind on some wildly dashing flight? She wondered if death were a warm place and if Friend felt safe there. She wondered how long her heart would feel this way.

Round Robin never learned what happened to Friend. Her wondering led her on to many places. She had long talks with owl, quiet sits with cheery creek and angry proud fights with rustling grass. Little by little Round Robin came to know something which has sometimes been called a great secret. Round Robin learned, almost by accident, what it is to love. By feeling her feelings for Friend, her longing and sad and mad and not-knowing, and by remembering the little laugh times, Round Robin began to feel a warm soft buzz in her own heart. Round Robin never learned what happened to her bird Friend. But now, deep within her own heart, her own self-friend had come home.

Coo-whit, coo-whit, coo-whit.

Annie Brook

A Sea Daughter's Gift

Today,
at dawn before sunrise
with full moon setting over the sea,
I walked along the seashore,
upon layers of golden sand deposited over time
concealing light from a world long ago

On this day
a mermaid called,
Morgan beside me again
mercurial and tumultuous,
singing up a sea dance for crashing waves
as moon and stars slipped deeper into their dark night

The air was wet and heavy
with whitecap foam and mist.
Glistening jewels of salt water
streamed down my face
softening an inflexible wound

My eyes turned
to tide-sown beds of whorled shells
sweet mysterious sea treasures
Cowrie, Calico Scallop, Coquina,
Conch, Coral, and Dark Cerith
But I left them untouched.

Instead, my tear-stained eyes sought out
white petal-faced sand dollars,
this mermaid's talisman.
A sea daughter's gift for those colorful souls
who will bring photos of art made long ago,
and stories of lovely friendships
where no mother lived

Today,
lying on wet sand
were hundreds of resonant reflections of the full moon,
and even though by any tally I am indebted,
I begged permission from Cliodhna
to carry those sun-bleached faces away
to serve them on a yellow platter that proclaims,
"When life gives you lemons, make lemonade"

My prayer today,
on the day of my Mother's memorial,
for Morgan and this sea daughter,
is one of gathering,
sanctification,
and release.

Susan O'Connell

What We Find When We're Leaving

At the end of your suffering
I found a missing moment
in your mind
of a time the waves washed in
gently, making moats for sandcastles,
and you took my tiny hand
in yours and we rushed
into the frigid fall Atlantic tide
with squeals and splashing,
without thought of what would happen
next, running out of the waves
while being chased by something softer
than our fears.

How I wish we could have stayed
there, where the earth was strong,
we felt free, and more than water
washed us clean.

When we thought together
we could stop it,
wanted to stop it,
tried to stop it,
would have stopped it
if we hadn't forgotten
what it was we were determined
to keep right in this world.

When we walked the shore
scooping plastic pieces of discarded
bottles into tiny blue pails

and you lovingly ran into the water
to catch the saranwrap floating
on the tip of a receding wave
as the lifeguard's whistle blew.

You swam back in, gathered me up
plastic in hand and whispered in my ear,
"today it's not just the children
who are over parented
yet so very unprotected."

Waiting to forget
what it is we have yet
to forget, you ask
if I remember,
and I wonder
how we finally find
a memory we both know
and see the same,

a moment when
we're still holding
one another,
still determined to right wrongs
whether or not they are ours,

a misplaced memory
that walked in
only to walk you home.

Maggie Mosher

The Angel of Death Passed Over You

The Angel of Death passed over you,
casting a shadow of much less substance
than the air through which it fell.
Whispering wings drove out my whisper's breath—
"Goodbye."
Your back has turned on now (and time),
your eyes see nothing
but the joyous journey home.

Shirley Harned

My Next Love

My next love
will be shameless;
careless, freewheeling, cartwheels of joy;
passion bursting with creative pleasure.

My next love
will be easy and painless.

My next love
will be an inheritance
of all that you, my lost beloved,
willed to me.

Maggie Jackson

Holding Your Voice

Holding
your voice
in my hands
your voice
given back to me
thirty years on
your voice, looped
reel to reel
turning me over.

Such a young man's voice
a tender tenor
breaking slightly
slow and soothing
reading our stories.

Leading us like Aslan
through the doorway into magic lands.
Pilgrims on a hazardous journey
via the *Slough of Despond*
to the *Delectable Mountains*.

Our faces rapt, absorbed
in the great mystery of words
beautiful, old-fashioned
piercing, potent
even to the edge of the *Black River*.

Not just the words themselves
but the sounds, the images
the tones of carefulness and care
and the silence
that wraps us close.

You gave us love.
Love and *hunger*.

Rosemary Palmeira

201

Time Passes

Years pass, decades. The road that we once had hoped to share with our loved one has taken twists and turns we never could have imagined. We've moved on, by choice or by necessity. But doing so doesn't mean that we have forgotten. So many years later, many of us still honor our lost ones with rituals, by visiting their graves, in our writing, or in our memories.

I contacted many of the contributors to the first edition of this book after nearly thirty years and asked them to reflect on the losses that had inspired their poems. What had they learned? How had losing and grieving their loved ones changed them? What has meaning now?

Some chose not to answer. Others, profoundly shaped by their grief in the ensuing years, engaged deeply with my questions. Some found gifts in their losses and wrote about appreciating the ways that their grief had changed them for the better. A few—especially those who had lost children—said that they still felt the sharp blade of grief from time to time, even as they, too, expressed gratitude for what they had gained in the wisdom that only loss can impart.

Woven through the tapestry of their answers were some common threads of growth and recovery: resilience in the face of more recent losses, compassion and empathy for others in grief, a greater awareness of life's fragility, and a continued, loving connection to the person they had lost.

This chapter shares the edited responses of seventeen contributors, along with some of their recent poetry.

203

Mara Teitel Sheade

My writing is probably what was most impacted by my brother Alan's death. As a child, I had wanted to be a writer but could never figure out what to write about. After Alan's death, I found a writing group that emphasized the free-writing approach; this process gave me a way in, and writing became my primary way of coping with his death and my grief. Over the years, I took many classes and workshops, and participated in other writing groups. Not only did this allow me to return to my childhood dream, it also helped me create a social network.

For many years it seemed like Alan and my grief were the only subjects I wrote about, but eventually I did start writing about other things. Over thirty years later, however, I'm amazed by how often my writing still returns to him, the night preceding his death, and my own grief. January, 2021 marked the 32nd anniversary of his death and my poem, *Your Ring*, was written only about a month earlier.

I used my writing experience to help others find their voices by leading my own workshops. I've worked in schools, libraries, and senior centers, as well as with frail and memory-impaired seniors. By leading workshops that focused on writing as a tool for healing, I was also able to "give back" to the Wellness Community (now Cancer Support Community) that supported my family through my brother's illness and death.

My experiences with grief have made me better able to support others coping with the loss of their loved ones. I have learned that grieving is a never-ending journey; the beginning can be a long, hard trek up the mountain but the terrain eventually smooths out, leaving only occasional rolling hills. Sharing that knowledge is the most valuable thing I can give to someone who is just starting that journey.

Having experienced this kind of grief prepared me for dealing with other types of grief and ultimately, the deaths of my parents. I knew, broadly, what to expect and how to be gentle with myself on the hard days. I knew not to buy into anyone else's definition of what was "normal" grieving.

I observe the traditional Jewish ritual of commemorating the anniversary of a loved one's death every year. After reading a brief prayer, I light a yahrtzeit (anniversary) candle, which is supposed to burn for at least 24 hours.

I was the only one with my brother on the last night of his life. For many years, I had a personal ritual of marking that anniversary by writing, sitting with thoughts of him, of that last night, and of how I'd changed in the past year. I used to do it without fail, and still try.

I gave my first child, a daughter, the middle name Alanna, in his memory. And sometimes, although it's not really a favorite of mine, I'll buy a slice of Alan's favorite birthday 'cake' (lemon meringue pie) to celebrate his birthday.

When my brother died, I rarely had the need to visit the cemetery. I felt that he wasn't really there. In the intervening years, both my parents died and were buried beside him. Now, I go more frequently, partly to carry on my mother's tradition (who would always go on birthdays and yahrtzeits, for both him and my father) and partly because now it feels like the place I can 'be with' my family. When no one else goes with me, I will sit there for a long time, look out on the rolling hills and trees, and write.

Your Ring (for Alan, 1953-1989)

I'm sure the metal remembers you
in its cold, uncompromising way.
Not like my memories which shift and alter,
creating their own realities.

I wear your ring, plain gold, your initials etched
on the simple, flat top in curlicue letters
which make them almost illegible.
If I stare long enough, though, they come into focus.

I really don't remember if you ever wore this ring,
but it is my keepsake of you. My talisman
that lets me believe you're still looking after me,
protecting me like a big brother should.

Maybe it doesn't have a memory of you;
its metal never bent to the shape of your finger.
But my flesh connected to your metal
fills the hole you left behind.

Mara Teitel Sheade

Watching the Yahrtzeit Candle Burn

1.

I sit in the dark
Writing by the flame of a candle
That burns a memory

I watch the flame dance with its reflection in the glass
They move as one but not together
The tangible heat, the crisp image
Taunted
By a glow just out of reach
There, but not really

2.

The flame burrows through 3 inches of wax, at least
    24 hours
The wax evaporates
Like memories you don't even notice are fading
A voice that barely whispers in your ear
You forget how the face has faded
Until you find the photo
She lives in a different place in your body
Sometimes, you forget the way there

3.

I am the flame
Dancing alone
Contained
I stretch and shrink
Bending to the will of the wind
I exist only for a day

Mara Teitel Sheade

Carlin Paige Holden

My friend Randy Harvey died on May 29, 1990, from AIDS, at age 36. I was 47. We had both volunteered for several years with Shanti Project, a grassroots AIDS service organization in San Francisco. I had already lost many other friends and acquaintances. When Randy died, I had to step back from direct service to people with AIDS and process my own accumulated losses. I attended the grief support group at the Center for Attitudinal Healing for a full year. It's been thirty years since he died and I clearly remember noting the retreat of this loss into the past, by days, then weeks, months, years.

I volunteered a few times with the AIDS Memorial Quilt and became aware of a new grassroots project in Golden Gate Park called the AIDS Memorial Grove. In 1993, I went to the Grove to commemorate what would have been Randy's 40th birthday. It happened to be the second anniversary of their volunteer workdays so there was a feast and celebration at midday. The Grove folks didn't care that I arrived late. They gave me a release form to sign and gloves to wear and sent me up a slope to pull elm tree suckers and blackberry brambles. I worked with a lively crew and was excited to return the next month and the next. I had found a new tribe.

In 1996, through congressional legislation, our local project became The National AIDS Memorial Grove, and in 2019 we became stewards of the AIDS Memorial Quilt as well. We are now known as The National AIDS Memorial.

I have continued to volunteer on workdays and to participate in other Grove activities for much of the last thirty years. I was surprised in 2011 to be invited to join the Board of

Directors. Though I'd never seen myself as a "BOD kind of gal," I decided to accept the challenge and I will complete my ten-year term at the end of 2021. To have contributed to the Memorial's evolution, from derelict acreage to a beautiful garden for healing and for joy, is beyond any dream I had ever had for my life.

One of Randy's gifts to me was to rekindle a childlike sense of wonder and magic at Christmas. He made me a gold brocade stocking—fabric from the ball gown we took turns wearing to Shanti volunteer parties in 1988. He also made sugar cookies cut into trees and stars. For many years I made cookies with his cutters and a set of Texas-themed ones to honor him and his roots.

My experiences around AIDS in the late 80s gave me a greater familiarity with death as a part of life, that there can be a lot of living in the midst of dying, that little ordinary moments can be the most precious freeze-frames of times together. I also learned that memorial services can be creative and that those are often more meaningful than one-size-fits-all religious rituals.

Remembering what was meaningful to me during times of grief, I am more sensitive to what might and might not be meaningful to others. I know that listening to a grieving person is more important than "trying to make them feel better," and I know better than to tell them how they must be feeling or that their loved one is in a better place or other presumptive cliches.

Light in the Grove

*"They are all gone
into the world of light..."*
          Henry Vaughn, c. 1652

Written in another land
and time of lives cut short,
centuries before
we claimed these acres.

Entering on World AIDS Day Eve
the glowing Grove,
their world of light,
a cloud of "fireflies" greets me,
Spirits hosting this magic.

Guests place candles
on names in stone,
resolving again
their story will live on.

Carlin Paige Holden

Sam Ambler

My grandfather died when I was five. My grandmother died when I was fourteen. My father died when I was twenty. My mother died when I was twenty-eight. My friends started dying when I was thirty-three and continued dying non-stop for more than a decade. My whole life, I have been surrounded by death.

And yet somehow, I was inoculated against it. I didn't really feel the death in my life until my best friend, Robert, died when I was forty-two. I moved in with him to take care of him. I held him as he passed. I felt his dead lover, Allen, come into the room with us, and I saw Robert leave his body out through his eyes and join together with Allen. And in that instant my life was transformed, in that instant I felt as though I had grown up at last.

The difference between a body animated by a spirit and a body that has been vacated is enormous, and incomprehensible until it is experienced. The two of them lingered for a while, saying good-bye to us. Then they crossed over out of my consciousness into whatever there is beyond. At that time, I became adamantly aware that death is not an end, but a doorway; that there is something on the other side.

And I lost any fear of death I may have harbored. The idea of death actually became a kind of comfort. I feel almost at ease now, as I move toward old age, buoyed by the lives and the loves of my chosen family and my blood family who have passed on before me.

Army of the Horsemen

They have been with us
from the very beginning,
the dead who haunt us,
the dead who hold our love,
the dead who help us
and trip us up.
All the love I feel
and have felt is rooted
in the love I found in my heart
for my dead Robert,
who raised me up, threw me aside,
and reached into that hole
to pull me out. For Allen,
who wanders still
in unmapped alternate dimensions.
For Chuck, who turned crimes
against nature into art and poetry.
For John Esther, who belly-danced
across Ishtar's altar into Astarte's
hoary realm. For Drew, who led
the chorus to Oedipal infamy.
For Misha, who was the well one.

For Rick, who married drag with life,
and lived! For Jimmy, whose shining
white hair gave luster
to his collection of antiques.
For Layton, who suffered so,
but smiled and laughed until he closed
his eyes at last forever.
For Sylvester, who rained love's confetti
onto adoring muscled sweating crowds
dancing at his feet. For Leonard,
who stormed the ramparts
of the armed services, who was
given a medal for killing two men,
and a discharge for loving one.
Oh Captain! My Captain!
Not much of a military man,
nor much of a captain,
but possessing such beauty, men follow—
I follow where you lead,
into the breach of the unknown—
holding hands, into the ephemerality,
not the finality, of death.

Sam Ambler

213

Rita La Bianca

My daughter, who we named Angela, was stillborn, so my loss is the loss of all the memories we never made over the past fifty years. At first, I thought it was fine. I had another child after my daughter died to prove I was not a freak. I had to prove to myself that I could have a healthy normal child after Angela and all her woes. I did have a perfectly healthy son already, but I blamed myself and thought it was my fault that my precious daughter had not made it past the first post.

My beloved Angela lives in my imagination. She never lived in reality. Her birth/death was the shattering of a million dreams we shared on our long, nine-month journey of swimming in turbulent waves which never reached the shore. I'm not sure there is a better place from here where we all eventually go, but I hope with all my heart her poor little broken body is whole again and she is dancing and laughing and watching over me.

I went to Angela's grave after I left the hospital, but it was not her grave alone. It was a mass grave, marked by a rusty, numbered plaque under which who knows how many tiny souls lay. How many had ceased living before they had drawn breath or soon thereafter? I cannot visit the dead in their graves since then. I pay my respects if I must, but I don't meander around cemeteries.

Time heals all and it did. But now in my twilight years, I look with envy at all those Mums and daughters doing their thing while I wish my daughter were here. The loss of my daughter taught me to be even more independent than I already was. I've had no daughter to egg me on or tell me how to dress or how I look, so hopefully, I've still made all the right choices—fashion-wise at least.

I've learned that in the end, we all need someone to love and be loved by. I have both in spades from my sons and four grandchildren. But the grandchildren have all grown up and have their own lives to deal with. I understand. My sons also lead busy lives, and sons love as sons love. They do not need a mother smothering them. Daughters, on the other hand, offer a different kind of love. I know because I am one. And I miss that experience more and more each day.

If Only You Were Here

We could talk
of the day I saw you walk down the aisle
of the moment I set eyes upon your just-born baby
white gouache vernix from head to toe
of babysitting through the years
and sharing tears when things got hard
of seeing your children
reach milestones like
kindergarten
university
first loves
and first heartbreaks

Of me growing old with you
doing all the mother/daughter things others do
even the occasional spat about nothing worth
    worrying about
We could talk
about your childhood tantrums
your beautiful hair
shining in the sunshine
of your first pair of heels
your skinny legs in tights
of everything and nothing
of silly things that by now we would have forgotten
except, my darling child
we did not get to share any of those memories

Fifty years do not dim your absence from my life
you're still my child, whose face I never saw
whose hair I did not touch
whose little fingers I did not count
before they whisked you away from me
on that cold August day

As if not seeing you meant I did not know you
my angel my Angela
with whom I shared each breath of my life
until it was time for you to slowly exit from
a warm place into the cold hard world
a world you were not meant to be a part of

If only you were here

to celebrate those five decades of life and living
with all its ups and downs
its happy times and sad
a life well lived
a life you loved
one I too could have loved with a light heart
instead of just remembering
all those moments I've lived without you

Rita La Bianca

Suzanne Fried-Freed

So much has changed since August 17, 1986 when my beloved brother, Richie, passed at the age of thirty-four from AIDS-related illness. I was thirty-six. Richie's passing brought me to my knees spiritually. I had to find a bigger purpose for my life than the way I was living at the time he left planet Earth. I was only a year into attending Al-Anon meetings at that time, and soon afterward, began attending other 12-step programs.

Soon after Richie's passing, I experienced very vivid visits from him in Spirit. One night a few months after his passing, the car was filled with the smell of his signature cologne, Polo. I was already familiar with the Other Side but the experiences of him in Spirit helped me through the darkness of the first few years as I wrestled with my despair and grief.

The degree to which we love is the degree to which loss tears us apart; Richie's passing shattered my heart. I miss him to this day and I know one day I will be reunited with him on the Other Side. I learned that the first two years of such enormous loss must be navigated with great self-compassion and tenderness; that we do survive, and in time, we can thrive and have a rich and fulfilling life. Finding meaning is the key to surviving any loss this Earth-walk throws our way.

After I graduated as a licensed psychotherapist in 1987, I thought I would work with people with HIV and AIDS. But I soon realized that was too close to home for me to manage. Instead, I channeled my insights from my journey of grief into facilitating grief groups in my practice and offering my Broken Hearted Way workshops to help others navigate the tsunami of loss.

There is always gold underneath the crap, to paraphrase Carl Jung; for me, the gold behind Richie's leaving was that nothing is too hard to do or say once you have gone through the hell of a loved one's torturous illness and the death.

Why not leap into your life and let the Divine carry you along on Her wings as you explore your talents? What is so bad about those leaps? What is the worst that will happen? Not death, that's for sure. Richie mined the depths of his talent on his short time on Earth. He inspired me to do the same as best I can.

In the last 20 years I have performed stand-up comedy, solo mini-performances at the Marsh Theater in Berkeley, California, and told stories at local MOTH events. Spiritual joy is tied to the innocence of a childlike wonder with the world. When Richie left me here on earth I had not a clue that one day I would share my wonder, my slanted perspectives on life, by performing in front of folks, telling stories to make them laugh and cry.

Freedom (for Missy Ida)

My mother
always knew when she left this
grief-filled Earth-walk
she would join her blonde, blue-eyed,
razzle dazzle
baby boy;
he 34 years grown a man
when death took him
granting
mercy
ending
the six month agony
through
the
twisting
corridors &
dead-end hallways
of AIDS
from diagnosis to
death.
For 15 years
after he left
she lived
cooking cleaning

learning to
rata tat tat
tap dance (like he did long ago
    in Clark studios New York City)
anything to fill the void.
Letting life
carry her
as she blessed us
with her wry humor,
shedding tears in private.

Two days after her memorial
The Twin Towers exploded.
On 9/12
I walked a deserted Florida beach
From
Nothing
Nowhere
No bird in sight
a
pelican
feather
drifted
down.

Suzanne Fried-Freed

Rosemary Palmeira

My dad died in 1963 at age thirty-six, when I was only eight. Going to another funeral recently—fifty years on—deeply affected me—being surrounded by people who knew my dad, seeing him through their eyes, feeling their empathy.

As a child psychologist, I am now horrified by the way my father's death was handled with us children. I was in a new country, home, and school, without friends or wider family. Many cultures allow drama, wearing black, closed curtains, armbands, shiva, keening, time out, the whole shebang. Wallowing even. At the very least, good loud noise and the community sorrowing with you. But Brits say, "Don't complain, don't make a fuss!" I wish I'd been given the chance to express my loss loudly and communally.

One lady noted my depression at the time and shared a verse from Psalms: *I will give you the treasures of darkness.* That really meant something to me. It's the only time I can recall someone trying to take my grief seriously, trying to put some meaning to it.

Our family never honoured anniversaries and I was never taken to my father's grave, though I occasionally went alone when I was old enough. I understand now the complex task a child must negotiate, caught between the need to keep her precious memory alive and the conspiracy of silence, even obliteration, that so many children suffer.

I realize now what I didn't before—that I am damaged and have symptoms of trauma. As a child, I wrongly imagined that other people felt as hollow as I did and didn't realize how different I was. I had almost no peers in a similar situation. Unconsciously, I felt—and still feel—unentitled, disinherited, self-deprecating, diffident and always an outsider.

All my adult phobic reactions seem to derive from unconscious childhood imprints. I understand now that my sense of dread relates to premonitions of fear: *something is about to go terribly wrong, and no one will tell me what it is.* I am an expert on shutting things down when I don't want to know or feel. But it certainly helps to identify what seems to be "the matter" with me, even this late in life.

I began to heal after having my first child. That happy baby gave me confidence to be a mother—it was new life for a lost one. And creativity was healing. For me it was my guitar, and poetry. Dylan, Simon, Mitchell and Cohen—my Mentors, my Truthtellers. And discovering poetry is what made me feel not so terribly alone.

When I look back on the child I was, that girl, and young woman, I see a remarkable person—courageous, determined to turn disaster into victory. I was a truth-seeker, lover of life and love, a yearner and creator. Despite tragedy, I have always known how to mine the rich veins of gold, the many flashpoints of joy. I have always been on a journey, reaching out to strays and strugglers.

What have I learned? That life, love, and people matter, but they are gifts, not entitlements. To pursue things that are life-affirming and mix with people who are life-giving, and to avoid or fight what is destructive. That, as the hymn says, "*This world is not my home, I'm just a-passing through.*" That there are still mysteries to come, things that we have not yet fathomed.

Forgotten Child

After many years I catch a glimpse—
fair ponytail and sea-green eyes,
dancing over the tawny boulders
spinning and spinning in the sunlight
white organza dress translucent
Who are you? Why can't I know you?

She runs to the door, beams at visitors,
gives bread to the gypsy mother and babe;
before the long voyage North
before the father's death, the chrysalis years
before reality breaks through, skin smarting.
Where are you now? How did I lose you?

Born at the mouth of the Douro
loves the river, loves the sea
throws herself full tilt into its roll,
its pebble-spitting, somersaulting delirium,
floats blissful on a giant inner tube.
Don't you know how much I've missed you?

In the walled garden, she plays in the slant
of shadow and light, sends Siamese kittens—
Hop, Skip and Jump—through nets and tunnels,
runs after Mischievous, the yellow duckling
not believing the day he turned white
lies in the belly of the playhouse roof.

Bright, pristine, innocent, whole
spinning and spinning across the sands
white organza dress translucent in the sun.
I see you now – you have come back to me.

Rosemary Palmeira

Dixie Thysen Laws

I made the image for this book (on page 91) after the death of my ex-husband. It was the first loss that was close to my heart. Since then, I have experienced many other losses— my parents, my brother, and even my own son.

Now I'm 75, and friends my age are passing away. It's always a jolt to lose someone close to me, but I know now that I won't feel bad forever, and there comes a time when grief turns into a sweet memory of the one that passed away.

So I just wait and go through my grief, and I am confident that I'll feel better about it eventually. I know I will have work to do to move along the path of grief: participating in funeral rituals, reading uplifting books, writing my thoughts, making art, getting out in nature to experience my place in the universe, and talking to others.

David C. Burke

I wrote my poem about my father as the AIDS epidemic was hitting. It's funny to reflect on him now in this pandemic. Grieving doesn't stop. It shifts and changes over time, as does the nature of my experience of my father, the way I hold him. Life changes me as much as I change my life. I'm in a different place than I thought I would be.

Grief doesn't transform. It is too much a part of us to be transformative. That would be like asking if birth transformed me. Grieving is part of the marrow of who we are. It is the denial of grief that transforms us...makes us less than. To numb the painful and what makes us vulnerable is to shut down what makes us alive. We can't just pick and choose. But I have learned that we never grieve alone.

I take from my father's life the things he was good at expressing. He tried to show people, especially strangers, that he was like them. I try to do the same even when it is an effort.

Mike Bernhardt

One evening in my bereavement support group, a couple of months after my wife Susan died, a woman spoke about how comforting it had been to be able to cry for her first husband in the presence of her new second husband. I told her that I hoped I might meet someone so tolerant of my love for someone else. She replied, "You won't settle for anything less."

I have been married for twenty-eight years to a woman I became friends with a few months after Susan died. Yvonne was patient and giving enough to let me grieve without demanding too much of me. At times it was very difficult for both of us, and it took time to build trust around my grief. When I was able to cry for Susan in Yvonne's arms, I knew I had found someone with whom I could make a lifetime commitment. At that moment I felt Susan joyfully give me her blessing.

As I grow older and look back at my life, I am awed by the unexpected twists and turns in my life's path. A chance meeting at a swimming pool while visiting Susan's best friend led to meeting Yvonne. I'd always wanted a child but Susan couldn't safely bear one; with Yvonne, I became a father. Falling off a ladder and breaking several bones led to a career change and financial stability for the first time in my life. Every step was an inflection point, though I didn't know it at the time.

I am brutally aware that it could all come crashing down. Few days go by when I don't remember that my wife or our son could die in a car crash, that I might die tomorrow and leave my family bereft. I don't lose sleep over it, but I know that life is fragile and everything can change in a moment. The reality of that is terrifying and sobering. I am grateful for what I have every day. I don't take any of it for granted.

Rose Drew

Before my daughter came, and went, I was one of the top salespeople at a very large department store chain. I sold kitchen appliances, like fridges and stoves, and laundry appliances. I worked hard, played pool, got drunk at the weekends. I was able to communicate with anyone who needed big, expensive machines for the kitchen or laundry room, and I treated all customers fairly. I joked around with my co-workers.

After Sarah died, I became more serious, more aware of the world. I left the sales job after the birth of my second daughter, and a back injury. Now I'm a special needs tutor; a science supply teacher; a forensic anthropologist, a performance poet; and a book publisher. I earned a master's at Yale; I moved to England for a doctorate. But many things are the same. I still "sell" school to doubtful kids, and books to readers. I treat people fairly. I joke with students, colleagues and other poets.

I am a teacher; a political activist; an anti-racist; someone who cannot see a wrong being done and stay silent. I am no longer able to sit and watch politicians do what they like. The world CAN be a better place. It is up to us.

I learned that life is unfair, it is short, and just because we want something to happen, very much, it does not always work out as we want it to. I'm sure I would have realized this by now. At age 29, I felt immortal. What could go wrong? Now I want to make every day count. I am filled with horror when someone's life is cut short for terrible reasons, such as the Syrian toddler drowned on a beach, who had died on the way to a safer life. We all deserve a safe place to live, food to eat, clean air to breath, fresh water to drink, the chance to work and play within a community. Because really, what else is there?

Elephant

You're still in the room;
the room's just larger.

Years spent ignoring you,
or else dragging out your secret life
the way a magician
flourishes bouquets from milk jugs: Ta da!
Now seen, then not,
enormous invisible reason for so much.

And time moves on,
events engulf a life,
one undersized elephant
gets pushed aside.
Soon enough, to trot you into view,
remove the camouflage
seems a petty, distracting trick,
or at least, too sad to mention.
Most people prefer a laugh
than to rehearse old sorrows.

But you've remained,
blended effortlessly in with houses and plans,
constant reminder that life
is too short
for injustice and squandered dreams.

You've always been here, in a room
that's grown to dwarf you, my elephant—
my mentor,
my muse,

it's me who has changed.

Rose Drew

Annie Brook

I was in ritual space for a whole year, a time out of time. Initially, I shaved my head and put Jac's ashes and my hair in the volcano in Hawaii. My heart needed so to feel and express such a loss. Jac's death threw me into an inquiry about grief, loss, love, and those forces that take us into the unknown.

Grief moments would seem to bubble up sometimes out of nowhere, so I learned to trust that and let them happen. Not wallowing, but allowing. It seemed to take about 20 years to feel my spirit fully returned, although I had explored other relationships. Now it is just a gentle smile, honoring what we shared. I find myself in gratitude often.

The same things that were important before Jac died are important to me now. Deep connection and meaning in life, creativity, the desire to be known and to know on that soul level. Honesty in speech and thought, warmth, humor. I miss some of the co-engagement of a shared vision path. However, I have learned to continue to foster and support my own vision.

I've learned how resilient I am. How curious life is. That there is only what is happening, not what we wish for. There is a knowing that comes with loss, and a sense of acceptance, and perhaps a trust in the process of moving on. I have gone on with my career in Somatic Psychology, developed my artistry in music and dance, and am writing more poetry. I have to make sure I don't compare my living life with "the road less taken" and what could have been. It has been a good lesson in valuing the present moment.

I wish I had understood the impact of shock. I might have made other choices immediately after Jac's death that could have helped me adjust more easily. I might have had the courage to face the financial planner and the wherewithal to manage the mortgage and finances of the home we shared, rather than having to sell it right away. That was a big upset.

Now understanding shock, I can see that this experience helped me research and develop protocols to help people come out of shock, whether event shock; or all the way back to that transition of soul into body that happens at birth; or the soul leaving the body, which was the gift in my experience of Jac's death. I learned what love really asks of us, to be open rather than grasping and holding on. This whole experience helped me create my *Birth's Hidden Legacy* books, and the foundation of my clinical work.

The greatest gift was seeing the room fill with Golden Light when Jac passed. We had given him water blessed by the Dalai Lama to open the gates of passage upon death. I think it worked; it was so comforting to think that he actually "made it home," and that all of us in the room were filled with awe and wonder witnessing this. It taught me what love really asks of one, and to see my beloved take such a journey, what more could I have wished for him!

Robin Lahargoue Shorett

My brother Mike passed away when I was only 12. While I was in middle and high school, I educated my peers about the consequences of drunk driving by giving schoolwide talks. Looking back, I'm completely baffled that I was able to do this. I'm in awe of my younger self. If I had to speak in front of the entire high school where I now teach, especially about painful memories, I'm not sure I could do it. But at the time, I felt it was my responsibility to do anything possible to prevent a similar tragedy.

Now I can see that it was an essential part of my grieving process. In fact, during high school, it was part of my identity. Eventually, I no longer wanted to be known for losing my brother. In college, I chose not to pursue this kind of public speaking. I did, however, share my story whenever I needed to ensure friends made the right decision about designating a driver. I still share his story (in less detail) with my students, in much smaller groups.

Being so young when Mike died, I don't know if I even knew myself yet. The loss of him is so embedded in my development, I don't think I can separate myself from it. I am confident that the loss of him at such a young age, aged me. In high school, I felt older than my peers. I knew a secret about life's fragile nature that other teens didn't yet understand.

Much later, as a new mother, I was hit very hard by the vulnerability of loving my newborn daughter, knowing that she could be taken from me any moment. It wasn't until I became a mother that I truly understood the depth of my own mother's loss when my brother passed. Losing a sibling is horrendous, but losing a child is an entirely different experience that goes against natural order. I named my second child, a boy, after my brother.

I've always felt that at my core, I am a person who keeps things in perspective. We all lose it once in a while, but in essence, I feel like Mike's death helped me really know what is important in life and what really isn't. It's one thing to intellectually understand that our loved ones shouldn't be taken for granted. It's another thing to know in your heart, to truly feel, that nothing and no one is guaranteed to be here for us tomorrow.

Lorene Jackson

I wrote my poem (*Until the Milk Stops*, page 10) at the raw beginning of losing my infant daughter Anna. Three decades later, it's still a journey. Yes, life goes on and it gets better. We recover in the short term; the raw pain moves into dullness and slowly fades into a safe fold in our hearts where we carry our loss and loved one with us for the rest of our lives.

After Anna died, I immersed myself in grief as much as I could, while still being there for my four-year-old son. I was also pregnant with my second son. Grieving the loss of a child tempered the excitement of having another. Would he be healthy? Once he was born, nine months from the day Anna died, life swept me along and I learned one of the first lessons of grief: I had to carry on.

When I was at my rock bottom, lying on the floor prostrate, unable to fight gravity any longer, I realized the best way to honor Anna was in the way I lived my life. That meant pulling myself together, being the best mom I could be, and living my best life. I always strived for that before Anna's death. But Anna gave me a stronger focus. Loss has a way of weeding out what's not important and strengthening our highest values.

I'm not sure there is ever an end to grief; there was no suddenly manageable day when I could breathe deeply once again. No single day when the tears stopped. But I do remember when I first really laughed again: about three years after my daughter died. I was on a Disneyland ride with my sons and I caught myself thinking, "Wow, I'm laughing again."

We honor Anna by keeping her memory alive. She remains a strong presence in our family, never forgotten, even by her two brothers who never met her. At Christmas, we used to hike to Anna's Grove where her ashes were spread and hang wooden heart ornaments in the overhead pine trees. Now, every year on her birthday, I hike to Anna's Grove or walk to the Compassionate Friends memorial where her name is on a stone plaque. I reflect on her life, grateful for the fleeting time we had. I think about how old she would be, but I can't reflect on what her life would have been. Who can know?

I am more empathetic. I'm able to reach out to others in their time of loss because I know how unbearably hard it is... forever. I gained confidence and strength knowing I survived. I learned resilience. I lost my innocence about what can happen in life. I don't take the health of my loved ones for granted. I found relevance in this saying: *You can't really laugh until you have cried.* I learned there is no threshold defining the loss or pain in our life.

There were things someone told me immediately after Anna died that helped me immensely. These are what I now offer my friends in their times of grief:

- Everyone grieves differently. In a marriage where two partners grieve separately, in different ways, it's important to respect one another's path and not be bothered if you don't match your partner's idea of what grief should be. If your partner says your grief is lasting too long, as hurtful as that can be, simply discount the comment.

- Some people will say unwittingly cruel and inappropriate things. Some things they say are just stupid, like, "It was God's will" or, "They were so young anyway." I would try to ignore these comments, file them in the "stupid things people say" file and let them fly away.

Paula Porter

I was 33 when I lost Jim, my husband of 13 years. In the 33 years since I found myself and my true passion. I have challenged myself in ways I never thought possible: I earned my master's degree and PhD, fell in love again, and after 23 years, became a widow again. It has now been 3 years since Dennis died. I thought that losing my second husband would be easier. That wasn't entirely true, though it helped that I was on a path I had previously walked.

After Jim died, a friend dragged me to a widows' support group. All of us were in our 30s, and our facilitator had lost her first husband in Vietnam. We had so much in common, yet never would have met had our husbands not died. Since Jim died on Christmas, I hosted my widow friends and their children for a remembrance dinner on that day, where we lit candles for our husbands. We all still do it every year.

I also started a commemorative Christmas tree with special ornaments for loved ones lost, including my dogs and horses. For Jim, there is a Harley Davidson motorcycle like we used to ride, and a single engine plane. I also hang his dog tags there. It brings me comfort when I go through this time of year.

Losing Jim opened new doors that I never would have expected to enter. I learned how strong I was when I fought the Veterans Administration (VA) to get Agent Orange survivor benefits. Jim was one of the first to die from his exposure and it took time for them to accept responsibility, but I won.

I used some of the VA settlement to go to Australia, where Jim had spent his leave from Vietnam. I really felt connected with him there. I slept on a cot in a tent for a month, explored the outback, the rainforest, and the Great Barrier Reef.

I also used the VA benefits to get my master's degree in Creative Writing, using poetry I wrote after Jim died as the basis of my thesis. I taught freshman English Comp classes, which rekindled my love of teaching.

While in college, I learned about computers and worked in a lab to help students with writing. I started exploring the nascent Internet, which led to meeting my second love online. The only issue was that he lived in Boston, 1500 miles away. We talked on the phone for hours. When he flew out to meet me, the chemistry we felt on the phone was still there, so after I completed my degree, I moved to Boston.

If Jim hadn't died, I likely wouldn't have gotten a master's degree, or found all the wonderful people whom I now call friends. I wouldn't have met Dennis, enjoyed living in the Northeast, or pursued my PhD in instructional design for online learning. And when Dennis died, I found a new life in Florida and new challenges, but I have continued to keep up with the friends and loved ones I have met along the way.

One thing that never changed is my love of horses and riding. These creatures have given me peace in times when I felt the lowest. And I continue to write as well as teach and work in the college classroom. I have become stronger in who I am and in my faith.

Graduating from the high school of grief has given me insights into myself, and the strength to move on with my life without questioning my choices. I have confidence in what I have done and can do. I learned that we can choose to be a victim and lose who we are in the throes of grief, or we can see doors opening for us that wouldn't have existed.

Sarah Rossetti

After my brother Simon died, we planted a Flame Tree on my property in rural Australia. We had a family service and buried some of his ashes with the roots of that tree. I feel like my brother now lives through me. Not like he was—a wound up stick insect who suffered depressive anxiety—but like someone at peace, who drops in from time to time to see how I'm doing. We called the tree Simon. May it outlive us all.

I listen for my brother's advice any time I need to ask, and I always know his answer, which soothes me. "Get in the pool," he'll say if I'm stiffening up from too many hours in my office. If I am suffering a break up, he will say with ironic knowing, "Love'll do it to ya!" Right after he died, I had to pull the car over as he said to me, "We used to fight, boy did we fight, but we really loved each other, aye." I tearfully replied, "Yes, we really did." I hold my brother in my heart like he never left.

I've learned to listen to depressed people, not advise. I've learned not to tell them the steps that I might take to get through stuff, because if s/he cannot make those steps, it doesn't help. Now I just listen and try to understand. I listen more than I talk now. Human beings seek connection and belonging with compassionate understanding—it's that simple.

My brother's death inspired me to live on no matter how bad anything gets, with more kindness in my heart, because we all struggle. We are all fallible, fragile human beings. I've just turned 59. My brother didn't make it to 59, and 2020—my 58th year—was a doozy, so I made it to 59 for us both, having learned resilience from my brother's death.

Cassandra English

Just like waves pounding against the shore, grief has pounded its way into my heart. At times, it has seemed like it would pull me under completely.

I was twenty. Standing over my sister's body, I began to cry, to cry really hard. The shock of her death hit me for the first time. "Not here" urged the nurse. I stepped outside, light was just beginning to flood the walkway. Side windows were reflecting a golden sunrise. It was so bright, so beautiful. I was furious and awestruck at the same time. How could this be?

My brother passed away soon after. I did not get to say goodbye. When we scattered his ashes, I felt lost. I remember gazing down at the ground. Amongst the river rocks, I saw a smooth heart shaped stone. I saw another, then another. All day long, I found them. It meant so much. I felt like he was there.

When my mother passed away, she was at home. I thought I was prepared, but is anyone prepared for their mother's death, really? On that day, I noticed the plum tree out front had just begun blooming. Soft pink colors and delicate flowers were everywhere. Once again, I was torn between my sorrow and the magical power of life. I resisted, but my mother's blossoming garden insisted. Within the week, two birds built a nest in the wreath on the front door, and I could see the baby birds through the peephole. Even now it makes me smile. Hi Mom.

As painful as my grief is, it continues to shape and change me. At moments, it still feels like a tumultuous wave threatening to pull me under. But in a heartbeat, it can yield. It can soften, and become a moment of calm, of stillness, and even, beauty.

Virginia Steele Felch

I was 42 when my beloved only child, Zach, died in an automobile accident on his way home from school at age 15. Our home burned to the ground not long after Zach died, along with all the memorabilia. That was really hard. I am now almost 75.

I have watched Zach's peers grow into adulthood as I had dreamed he would. Jobs, marriages, and children. I deeply grieve not having his children to love and stories to share with my friends. When my friends talk about their grandchildren it is challenging and sometimes heart-piercing. I have to pretend I'm OK, even though I am truly happy for them.

Over the years, being open and forthcoming about my loss has caused people to almost turn white and become silent. *Do you have children?* Answer: *I have two stepchildren and I lost my only child when he was 15.* End of conversation. Once, on maybe the third anniversary of Zach's death, I was having lunch with friends and expressed my sadness. One of them retorted, "Don't you think it's time to get past that, Ginny?" So many experiences like this. I have become a bit of a hermit, hiding out to be safe with my feelings and my loss, not wanting to risk being misunderstood or being hurt. I know I am not alone in this. Many parents who have lost a child experience similar reactions. We become silent warriors.

I have symptoms of post-traumatic stress, like anxiety and distrust and hypervigilance. I think of myself as a warm, sensitive and emotional woman. Even my good friends say they can't believe how warm, kind and passionate I am. Yet I feel as though I have a shell, a mask, where tears rarely penetrate. When they do, I feel grateful for the current of emotion streaming through my body like a soft relief.

I do have some dear friends to whom I can reveal my sadness without fear. I am grateful for that. And I have a precious husband—not Zach's dad, but we had just gotten married when Zach died, and the two were close. He loves me deeply, even when I am grieving. We have traveled extensively and I have lit candles in churches and shrines all over the world. I have laughed and partied with friends and enjoyed those times when I could slip out of the shell and feel soothed and safe.

I feel so much maternal love. From day one, I mothered dolls, dreamed of babies, and babysat as much as I could, pretending those children were my own. I became a children's photographer because my heartfelt imagery was appreciated. What does one do with this maternal drive/instinct?

The saving grace of grief and loss is the gratitude that I feel and express for the smallest things: the smell of pavement in the first rain of the season, the chirping of birds in the spring, the ocean roaring, my husband's smile.

Zach and I shared a deep love of our standard poodles. We played, ran with them, giggled and talked funny doggy talk with them. To this day I behave similarly, if not so athletically. I cherish this and think of Zach joining me in some way. And I can still see the glint in Zach's eyes, his teenage mocking humor, his beautiful thick blond locks, his love of photography, his mischievous antics. Sometimes that makes me laugh and other times my chest clamps up and my heart aches.

The deep spirituality and faith I experienced after Zach died has greatly lessened. But I do still hold on to the fantasy that I will see him when I pass, and we will be together again.

Artwork Credits

Page xxii
Cassandra English: *Opening*, colored pen and pencil

Page 7
Cassandra English: *Flight*, pencil and ink

Page 33
Nickie Zavinsky: *No!*, pen, brush and ink

Page 61
Cassandra English: *Reaching*, photograph

Page 91
Dixie Thysen Laws: *Shadow Person*, print from cut linoleum block

Page 125
Cassandra English: *Sister Dream*, pencil and ink

Page 135
James L. Carcioppolo: *Man Alone*, print from cut linoleum block

Page 165
Catherine Firpo: *Hummingbird's Flight to the Moon*, pen and ink

Page 202
Yvonne Lefort: *A Wintry Day*, 35mm photograph

Page 245
Cassandra English: *Connected*, photograph

Page 268
Cassandra English: *Miss You*, photograph

About the Contributors

Following are short biographies of the contributors to this book. Of the original forty-five people who contributed to the first edition, at least four have died; I was unable to locate ten others. The bios that have not been updated in some way are marked with an asterisk (*). There are thirty-eight new contributors to this second edition.

Sam Ambler's best friend of 17 years, Robert, died of AIDS in 1992, and he lost many other friends as well. His poems were published in a number of journals and he was also a winner of the San Francisco Bay Guardian Poetry Contest in 1991 and 1993. After a long career in theater, Sam retired in 2019 and is once again focusing his energies on poetry. You can read about his current thoughts on grief in the "Time Passes" section of this book. *(pp. 10, 96, 130, 211, 212)*

Anonymous: This contributor chose not to publicize his name. His wife died of cancer in 1991. When she died, their four-year old daughter kissed her goodbye and said, "When the spirit dies, the body's no fun." As a result of his experience, this contributor, a psychotherapist, began facilitating groups for cancer patients and their families. *(p. 146)*

Jodie Appell's sister Laurie died of COVID-19 in the spring of 2020. Despite suffering with mental illness and hallucinations, Laurie won a Connecticut "Governor's Victory Award" for her work in mental health advocacy. She loved to read and write poetry. Jodie was a singer/songwriter at a young age, studied semiotics in college and then sang in a jazz trio until she became ill with Lyme disease. When Jodie was eight, a teacher told her to stop writing poetry. She has been writing poetry ever since. *(p. 100)*

Paco-Michelle Atwood lost her father to COVID-19 while she was quarantined and recovering herself. She promised herself that she would honor both that experience and her father as soon as she was able to write about them. Paco-Michelle is a poet and mixed reality content producer with a professional background in technical quality and creative development. She focuses on supporting the arts, alternative healing, and self-empowerment. *(p. 84)*

Jill Iris Bacharach wrote *centerpart* for her grandfather, although she also was very affected by the death of a good friend in 1992. But her greatest loss was when her grandmother died in 2003, someone with whom she had shared a deep, soul-level bond since early childhood. Everything that matters to her, she learned from her grandmother. She says that it took her over ten years to recover from that loss. Jill wrote, "The reality is that nothing in life is ever ours; nothing is guaranteed. Nothing." *(p. 172)*

Mike Bernhardt, editor *(pp. 8, 40, 116, 127, 153, 161, 190, 228)*

Annie Brook's husband died suddenly with undiagnosed leukemia four months after they got married. Annie said that she has learned to "let the past rest in its sacred place, remembering it but not holding it in front of me." You can read much more about her current thoughts on grief in the "Time Passes" section of this book. *(pp. 37, 108, 137, 192, 232)*

Kathleen Browning wrote her poem for her eldest brother and sister, who were anchors for the five siblings after their parents died decades ago. Her brother died in 2020 from lung cancer induced by Agent Orange. Her sister died a few months later. Her sister didn't contract COVID-19, but she died because of a lack of effective medical care due to the pandemic. The pandemic also prevented Kathleen from traveling to help scatter her brother's ashes. The family held a memorial service on Zoom. *(p. 68)*

David C. Burke is a social worker. He decided to work with HIV and AIDS patients after his father's death in the 1980s, and then left that work five years later as his personal grief work also seemed to come to an end. He had not shared *Eulogy For My Father* with anyone until reading the notice for this book. It was written just after David's father died, but with healing, he felt that he might have written it differently. You can read about his current thoughts on grief in the "Time Passes" section of this book. *(pp. 98, 227)*

Tim Cannon has lived with direct knowledge of an incident—still considered classified information—that resulted in the deaths of some men during the Vietnam War. Because the event was classified, he was not allowed to tell anyone what happened. His poem was written after his only visit to the Vietnam Memorial in Washington, D.C., and it was the only piece he wrote about his experiences in Vietnam. *(p.152)* *

James L. Carcioppolo began his art career on his return from Vietnam and graduated from the San Francisco Academy of Art in 1976. The piece included here is part of a book in pictures entitled *From the Darkness*, in which he expresses his feelings about grappling with the losses in his life. He has since written several books, including *The Papyrus of Sek*, a fully-illustrated poetic journey based on ancient Egyptian texts. *(p. 135)*

Dale Champlin's mother was a joyous presence until her death. Dale's childhood summers were spent with her mother and three younger sisters in the idyllic, natural beauty of Upstate New York. Dale is the editor of *Verseweavers*, an annual anthology of prize-winning poems from contests sponsored by the Oregon Poetry Association. She published her first collection, *The Barbie Diaries*, in 2019 and has three more coming. *(p. 154)*

Cathleen Cohen wrote her poem for a close family friend who died of a heart attack in the summer of 2020. The family was fortunate to be able to hold a socially-distanced, outdoor funeral during the pandemic. In her late sixties, Cathleen has had other losses and finds

248

that writing and painting are helpful for expressing her grief. "There is a Jewish saying when someone dies," Cathleen said. *Let their memory be a blessing.* "During the pandemic, I find that distancing, isolation, and a different sense of time passing have caused me to embrace these memories more than before." *(pp. 70, 102)*

Monica Jean Davis found her mother dead, a suicide victim, when she was fifteen years old. She later dealt with several other deaths, three divorces and multiple miscarriages. As an adult "filled with a child's grief," she said that the most important thing in her life was her quest for inner peace and healing. Writing was an important part of that process. Monica was a registered nurse. She passed away in 2015. *(pp. 36, 57, 141)*

Rose Drew's first daughter Sarah died in 1989 from Sudden Infant Death Syndrome. Rose had previously loved to write, but she couldn't for many years after losing Sarah. Hearing that Rose had once written poetry, a neighbor encouraged her to attend an open mic event. A few months later, Rose began to write again. Aside from writing, she now runs a small publishing company. You can read more about what Rose has learned in the "Time Passes" section of this book. *(pp. 103, 158, 229, 230)*

Cyra Sweet Dumitru, a poet and a practitioner of poetic medicine, is part of a counseling team that works with health care professionals traumatized by their work during the pandemic. *Swimming the Cathedral* was written to honor the fear and grief expressed by a nurse who had been witnessing, for months, the suffering of people hospitalized with COVID-19. The italicized words in her poem quote the nurse directly. The poem gave her a way to lighten her own grief and "to bear witness to his suffering even as he witnesses the suffering of others." *(p. 88)*

Cassandra English has relied on her artwork as an important means of self-expression. When she was a young adult, Cassandra lost her sister, her brother, and then her mother. These losses changed her forever, opening her not only to heartbreak but also to life. She is now a fourth grade teacher as well as a multimedia artist. You can read more about her journey in the "Time Passes" section of this book. *(pp. xxii, 55, 119, 228, 241, 245, 268)*

Carla Halversen Eskelsen is a musician and songwriter. The title of her poem, *Nothing Like the Sun*, is also the title of an unfinished play written by her close friend Doug, who died in 1988 (the quote at the beginning is from the play). Carla has been married to her songwriting and performing partner for over 43 years. They have five children, five grandchildren, and a revolving assortment of horses, dogs and cats. *(p. 110)*

Renee Esposito was four years old when her father died from a heart attack in her presence. Because her family was unsupportive at that time, it was only in her late forties the she was able to begin working through her grief. She contributed her recent poetry to this book because she knew that honoring her father and her inner work in this way would help her heal. *(p. 140)* *

Virginia Steele Felch was a nationally-acclaimed children's photographer before her fifteen-year old son was killed in a car accident in 1990. Afterward she decided to use her talents to help transform societal norms regarding grief. "Our culture should teach us to be open and supportive," she said. "But instead, it teaches us to be positive and strong or much worse, to ignore grieving people completely." You can read more about her thoughts in the "Time Passes" section of this book. *(pp. 53, 242)*

Catherine Firpo's father died in 1989, and each year on his birthday, she goes to a beautiful place in nature and plants a tree. She has taught meditation and art to adults as well as children. Catherine is an exhibiting and published artist whose watercolor paintings have appeared on several book covers. She also has a PhD in Psychology and teaches the subject as an adjunct professor at two community colleges. *(pp. 156, 165, 166)*

John Fox's sister Holly had a way of defying stereotypes, even the sweet stereotype of a person with Down syndrome. Until her death at sixty-three, Holly was brilliant, unusual, stubborn, surprising, deep and funny. John felt a call to poetry at the age of 13, and his life has been an unfolding response to that call. A genetic disorder called neurofibromatosis impacted his right leg at the age of four. After fourteen years of multiple surgeries and hospitalizations, that leg was amputated below the knee. Learning to live with apparent imperfection, John believes tuning into beauty (along with the companionship of poetry and the sacred place it provides) serves as his main medicine and lasting inspiration. *(p. 174)*

Michael Frachioni's mother spent her last hours almost exactly as he described them in his poem. An attorney by profession, he spent his daily bus commute reading and writing poetry until the pandemic arrived. He is active with a regional poetry group, participating in and hosting poetry events in the area, and he has had several of his poems published. *(p. 29)*

Suzanne Fried-Freed's poems were part of a manuscript she published called *Loving Richie*, which was about growing up with her brother, his AIDS diagnosis and eventual death, and her life after his death. She also published many other works of poetry and non-fiction. Suzanne was a psychotherapist specializing in loss and grief. She now works as a clairvoyant psychic. You can read about her current thoughts on grief in the "Time Passes" section of this book. *(pp. 48, 54, 117, 218, 220)*

Robert Fulkerson's adoptive father killed himself when Robert was an infant. He was a senior in college when he contributed his poem to the first edition of this book, longing for the father he never knew. When his adoptive mother died a few years ago, he began a journey to understand how his past impacts his present. He says that although the poem is an accurate snapshot of where he was then, he has a profoundly different understanding of who he is now. Robert teaches computer science at a university. *(p. 148)*

Gill Garrett was in her twenties and working as a nurse when her mother died unexpectedly. She was devastated but had little time to grieve as she took over her disabled father's care, married, raised children, and worked as a health-care writer and lecturer. It is only now, forty years later, that she has truly been able to come to terms with her loss. She has found writing about it to be very therapeutic, and that the grief from so long ago is "resurrected with amazing clarity." *(pp. 28, 44)*

Deborah Eve Grayson lost her older brother to cancer in May 2020. Though she was extremely close to him—"my first friend"—she could not be with him or even contact him due to the pandemic. Afterward, she and her family could not sit shiva or hold a funeral. Even though she has had a long career as a mental health counselor specializing in bereavement, the circumstances have made grief difficult. Deborah says she has always written poetry. She was also a Poetry Therapy Mentor for the National Association for Poetry Therapy. *(pp. 26, 74)*

Margaret Grote was very ill and close to death at one point in her life. She came to depend heavily on a friend to whom she feels she owes her recovery. Her poem was not written about an actual death, but about her fears of the possibility of losing people like her friend. Margaret has been writing poetry for most of her life, and her work has appeared in several magazines. She also published a collection of her own work called *Going Home. (p. 38)* *

Jan Haag wrote *Canary Bird Zinnias* for her close friend and colleague, Pat Schneider, who died in August 2020. Pat developed the Amherst Writers & Artists method, which is used around the world to support writers in finding their own voices. Jan, a writing professor, created a college course based on AWA. A former newspaper journalist and magazine editor, Jan is the also the editor of AWA Press, and she leads writing workshops using the AWA method. *(p. 181)*

Julie Hagie's older brother died in a car accident when she was six, her best friend died when she was in her teens, and later, her younger brother died in a house fire. Her poems in this book came out of those losses. More recently, losing her parents, especially her mom, has been very painful. Julie has been drawing, painting, writing poetry, and keeping a journal for most of her life. She raised four children and has multiple grandchildren. *(pp. 59, 94)*

Debra Ann Halloran is the youngest sister of contributor Monica Jean Davis, who died in 2015. Debra knew little of Monica's many losses because they had been estranged. After receiving a copy of the first edition of this book, she wrote her poem *A Sister's Response*, which appears right after one of Monica's poems. Between 2008 and 2019, Debra lost her father and all three of her siblings to various illnesses. *(pp. 22, 142)*

Shirley Harned had many losses in her life, including her mother and many close friends. She said that though she often tried to avoid dealing with grief by keeping busy, doing so only delayed the process and made herself "tired, depressed and irritable in the interim." Shirley was a professional opera and concert singer, as well as a voice teacher, when she submitted her poem. *(p. 198)* *

Merna Ann Hecht works as a poet and storyteller with youth who have experienced life-changing loss and trauma. The year of isolation that the pandemic has brought to these young people has furthered her awareness of the collective sorrow we all carry. The presence of so much loss prompted her to write her poem, *To Hold the Loss*. Merna meets on Zoom with groups of all ages—writing with them to give voice to both solace and grief—which she describes as a hope-filled practice. She has lost dear friends, who were young and vital in their lives and life-work, to cancer. *(p. 62)*

George Hersh struggled to deal with the death of his father from cancer and the suicide of one of his sons—made much worse because they both occurred in the same month. As a result of that experience, George decided to retire from his previous career and pursue a PhD in psychology. He was proud to have been credited as the geomancer for Ursula LeGuin's book, *Always Coming Home*. George died in 2015. *(p. 112)*

Carlin Paige Holden has lived in San Francisco for much of her life. She had already experienced a number of losses when she wrote about the death of her friend and soulmate Randy, who died from AIDS in 1990. Carlin has volunteered for decades with the National AIDS Memorial and currently serves on its board of directors. You can read much more about her in the "Time Passes" section of this book. *(pp. 95, 128, 208, 210)*

Talitha Anne Hostetter wrote *Christopher* for her niece and niece's husband. Christopher was to be born twenty-one years after his parents were told that it was impossible for them to have another child, but he died two weeks before he was due. Talitha said she likes to write "when I am especially moved by life, be it sad or joyous, beautiful or ugly." *(p. 169)* *

Lorene Jackson's daughter Anna died in 1989 from a congenital heart defect at the age of seven months. Lorene wrote two children's books exploring sibling grief, and a collection of prose and poetry called *Never the Same*. Lorene has a master's degree in Public Health and spent many years raising two sons as a stay-at-home mom. You can read more about Lorene's thoughts about grief in the "Time Passes" section of this book. *(pp. 16, 236)*

Maggie Jackson and her partner Tim lived together for twenty-five years and for half of that time, Tim endured chronic ill health. After he died, grief inspired her writing of poetry, vignettes, monologues and reflections, which many people found helpful. She had the privilege of being "Poet in Residence" at an Anglican monastery and published *Offertory*, a collection of poems, from that beautiful experience. Ten years after losing Tim, Maggie says that life is meaningful and fulfilling again, but she still feels incomplete without him. *(pp. 122, 199)*

Jill Jennings lost both of her parents, her ex-husband, and her great-aunt within a sixteen-month period. Later, her stepfather died and just recently, her stepmother. In each case, the body was taken for cremation before she knew the person had died, and her desire to be present at the cremation was sometimes ridiculed. Jill is a retired teacher and journalist who, in normal times, organizes poetry slam events at her local high school. *(pp. 46, 114)*

Kathleen M. Johansen was eighteen years old when she wrote *Letter to Adam* to a close friend after Kathleen's brother, Paul, died of cancer. She was a participant in one of the first emotional support groups for children at the Center for Attitudinal Healing, run by the late Jerry Jampolsky. Kathleen helped produce one of the books published by the Center called *Straight from the Siblings: Another Look at the Rainbow. (p. 120)* *

Jazz Jaeschke Kendrick lost both of her parents and her aunt, who was like a mother to her. But nothing prepared her for her son's death from a glioblastoma in August, 2020. Along with grief came gratitude that she could help him through his last months. Grief has become her spiritual companion shaped her outlook on everything. Jazz discovered her own inner poet when her young daughter began asking her to spell-check her own poems. *(p. 168)*

Elizabeth Kuykendall wrote *Someone Died Today* after her brother, Matt, died from AIDS in 1991. As his primary caregiver, she initially felt isolated and angry at how quickly people forgot her brother and expected her to do the same. Matt's death helped her become stronger and gave her a more well-rounded, less naive view of the world. She has since raised two daughters who are now grown. *(p. 12)*

Rita La Bianca carried grief from the stillbirth of her daughter, Angela, for twenty years until she began to heal as a result of writing about it. "No one understands how inadequate, unclean, abnormal a mother feels for producing a less than 'normal' child," Rita wrote. She later supported other women living with maternal grief by helping them to talk and write about it. You can read about how she feels now about her loss, fifty years later, in the "Time Passes" section of this book. *(pp. 19, 214, 216)*

Dixie Thysen Laws is an artist and print maker. Her ex-husband died soon after their divorce. Dixie's work has been featured in group and one-person art exhibits throughout the United States, and her pieces have been purchased by several corporations, including the State of California. You can read about her current thoughts about grief in the "Time Passes" section of this book. *(pp. 91, 226)*

Yvonne Lefort's mother died from lung cancer in 1989. Yvonne was ambivalent at first about sharing *The Aftermath*. But after writing it, and with support, she worked through her anger and felt much more compassion toward her mother. She hopes that her poem will help people understand how the devastation of war can scar future generations through "inherited" grief. Yvonne is a career counselor and a multi-lingual, intercultural trainer. She also happens to be married to this editor. *(pp. 56, 202)*

Dorothy Lemoult wrote her poem after the suicide of a very close friend a few years ago, but she has revisited it many times during COVID isolation. She is a French-American multi-disciplinary artist and psychotherapist. She embraces the arts, community, and non-violent communication practices as ways to promote resilience, health and social justice. Dorothy studied poetry with John Fox at the Institute for Poetic Medicine for 3 years but her greatest life teacher is her son, Elliott, currently 8 years old. *(p. 138)*

Wendy Lichtman is a freelance writer and journalist. She has written five books for children and young adults, including *Secrets, Lies, and Algebra* and a children's book on grief entitled *Blew and the Death of the Mag*, which she wrote following her mother's death. Her essays have appeared in local and national magazines and newspapers. *(p. 184)*

Victoria MacDonald was fifteen years old when her father died. She was not included in the "grownup world" of her father's death and felt that her entire life had been shaped by her struggle to deal with the deep alienation she felt. She wrote *Daddy Love* as an adult after hearing of my search for poetry for the first edition of this book. Victoria has facilitated support groups for children who have lost a parent, and she also teaches dance. *(p. 58)* *

Kitch Martin had lived next door to Chet and his wife for three years when Chet died from Covid. His death triggered the grief Kitch feels for her own sister's suicide in 2010, which she still struggles to process. That older grief helped her to appreciate the long, difficult road Chet's wife would have to walk, and they have become good friends. Kitch calls herself a "recovering academic" who loves to write, and she "luxuriates" in art and poetry. *(p. 71)*

Claudia McGhee's partner of fifteen years, Karl, died from lung cancer in July 2019. Claudia was his primary caregiver and afterward, as she struggled with grief and exhaustion, the pandemic arrived. Lacking a "pod" or nearby family has exacerbated her grief. Claudia has dealt in words for decades as a software technical writer, newspaper columnist, editor, eBook producer, poet, and fiction writer. Her poems have appeared in a variety of print poetry journals and anthologies. *(p. 52)*

Elizabeth McMahon's father died in October, 2020 as his wife of seventy-one years held him. He served in the Navy during WII, including at the Battle of Iwo Jima, and later became a physician. He was buried with full military honors at Arlington National Cemetery. Elizabeth is a psychologist who works to relieve fear and anxiety using innovative techniques like Virtual Reality. She loves that words and music have the power to move people deeply. *(p. 86)*

Sharon R. Micenko wrote her poem on the tenth anniversary of a miscarriage that she had in 1982. She says that no one took her miscarriage seriously, and she was just told to forget it and try again. Though she eventually had four more children and no one else seemed to remember her miscarriage, Sharon never forgot that she might have had five. She lives in Western Australia. *(p. 109)*

E. Ethelbert Miller wrote his poem after the twenty-five-year-old son of a good friend ended his life on New Year's Eve, 2020. Ethelbert is a renowned writer and literary activist whose poetry has been translated into nearly a dozen languages. He is a two-time Fulbright Senior Specialist Program Fellow to Israel and has taught at several universities. He also hosts a weekly radio show in the Washington, DC area. His 2005 poem honoring HIV/AIDS caregivers, *We Embrace,* is engraved on the pavement surrounding a circular bench outside the Dupont Circle Metro station in Washington, DC. *(p. 39)*

Caryn Mirriam-Goldberg has been leading writing workshops and retreats since 1992 for adults in transition, people living with serious illness, and intergenerational and multi-cultural groups. During the pandemic, she has been leading her writing workshops on Zoom. She was inspired to write her poem, *Your Grief for What You've Lost,* during a workshop with twenty participants dealing with grief and serious illness. It was inspired by the many losses in her own life and in the lives of the people she supports. Caryn was the Kansas Poet Laureate from 2009-2013. *(p. 106)*

Maggie Mosher lost a number of friends to the Covid pandemic. As a young girl, she spent time with Mother Teresa on the Navajo reservation in New Mexico. It changed her life. Maggie has been a hospital and nursing-home volunteer since she was twelve and has been teaching children with special needs for over twenty years. She says, "We are all going through something difficult, something hard to express and even harder to live. Poetry gives me hope that I didn't even know I needed. The writings of others help me feel less alone, and I hope mine does the same for others." *(pp. 72, 76, 196)*

Christie Mudder's girlfriend Sandy was diagnosed with a brain tumor only two months after had they met. Sandy's health deteriorated just as the pandemic arrived, and Christie was pushed out of their shared home by Sandy's family and friends. When Sandy died a few months later, in the middle of the pandemic, Christie was left to grieve alone and she has struggled with the isolation. Christie has loved reading and writing poetry since childhood. She majored in English in college and since retiring, has focused on writing her own poetry again. *(p. 78)*

Dawn Nelson was a massage therapist when the first edition of this book was published. Her specialty, providing "touch therapy and gentle massage to those who are less active, aging, ill and/or in later life stages," took her on many visits with clients who were in hospice care. *Eileen* was written about a particular client she had worked with and grown to love. Between 2005 and 2007, she lost several of her own relatives and loved ones. *For Aunt Bobbie* was written after the death her favorite aunt. *(pp. 51, 175)*

Chike M. Nzerue was born in Nigeria and is now a physician in the USA. His brother died from Covid-19 in Nigeria, in January, 2021. Chike also lost a cousin, an obstetrician in New Jersey, who became infected with Covid while performing a caesarean section—mother and child lived, but his cousin died. And he will never forget the face of the patient he describes in his poem *Silent Hypoxia*. Chike has always loved reading and writing poetry. He says that when the grief becomes unbearable, he goes to two poems he loves: *Earth to Earth* by Kalu Ukah, and especially Phillip Levine's *You Can Have It. (pp. 66, 83)*

Susan O'Connell's brother-in-law died just as the pandemic began. The isolation has made it difficult to deal with the loss, as well as to support her brother-in-law's widow in the way she would have liked. *The Sea Daughter's Gift* was written for her mother, who died in 2014. *In Bud* was written for her brother-in-law a month after he died. Susan also lost her father and several friends. She is an expressive arts therapist and was co-chair of the International Expressive Arts Therapy Association. *(pp. 191, 194)*

Shannon M. Pace had longed to be present at the end of her grandmother's life. But because Shannon's mother was sick with Covid and her husband was a nurse caring for Covid patients, it wasn't safe for her to visit when the time came. Shannon crafted her first poems around age eight on an old typewriter in her grandmother's attic, and later earned her MFA in Poetry. She is a mother to three boys and loves hiking in the woods near her home, where nearly all of her poems come to her. *(p. 30)*

Rosemary Palmeira was very close with her father, but was not given any support after he died when she was eight years old. She spent much of her life feeling like she was carrying a "Monstrous Secret" that no one would understand. After her first child was born, twenty-two years later, she finally found the courage to ask for help. Rosemary has been a therapist, social worker, teacher, translator, and widely published writer. She is now a child psychologist who works primarily with refugees and asylum seekers, "paying it forward." You can read more about her journey in the "Time Passes" section of this book. *(pp. 14, 200, 222, 224)*

Dixie Pine said that she never was very spiritual until her brother Doug took his own life in 1991. After that, forgiveness became an important part of her life. In addition to writing, she also found creating visual art to be a powerful creative outlet, despite the fact that she had not drawn anything since childhood. *(pp. 50, 136)* *

Kirsten Porter's cousin died suddenly and unexpectedly in his early forties, alone in his apartment during the pandemic. Her family's grief was compounded by the safety restrictions of the pandemic, which prevented them from gathering together for the funeral and to try to make sense of their loss; they had to grieve apart. Kirsten is a freelance editor, poet, professor, and guest lecturer. Her work focuses on women, cultural diversity, community, and the ability for all to repair what is broken in themselves and the world. *(p. 82)*

Paula Porter lost her husband in 1987 to cancer caused by exposure to Agent Orange during the Vietnam War. Her poetry became so important to her that she completed a master's degree in creative writing, using her own poetry as the basis for her thesis. She also wrote a novel based on her experiences in a grief support group for women. You can read more about how her life has changed since losing her husband in the "Time Passes" section of this book. *(pp. 113, 123, 126, 147, 238)*

Elspeth Monro Reagan, MD was a pediatrician and psychiatrist in New York City. Her daughter took her own life in 1981 after a long struggle with severe depression and anorexia. Elspeth's husband left two years later. She felt that her experiences made her much more effective and compassionate in her work with patients. *(p. 49)* *

Frances Richey was a hospice volunteer in New York City when she wrote *Dear Mark* about a patient, an artist who touched everyone with his spiritual transformation in the last months of his life. Because of what he taught her, she was able to give much more to her other patients. She said, "Love can happen in an instant." *(p. 176)* *

Sarah Rossetti's brother killed himself in 2016; she wrote *Brother* on the day she learned about it. *Quiet Rooms*, which appeared in the first edition of this book, was written with her friend Rita La Bianca to "break the taboo" that (still) surrounds maternal grief for stillbirth and miscarriage. Although she never lost a child, she worked extensively with grieving mothers to help them express their pain through writing. Sarah is a published writer and screenwriter who lives in Western Australia. You can read about her thoughts on grief in the "Time Passes" section of this book. *(pp. 19, 25, 240)*

Nori J. Rost considered herself a "grief expert" until her brother, Erik, took his own life in 2013 at the age of fifty-five. She discovered that surviving his suicide was far more dense, dark, and despairing than any other grief she had experienced. Prior to that, Nori lost her dad to cancer and a nephew to SIDS. During the AIDS epidemic, she lost thirty-three friends and officiated at scores of memorial services. Poetry has been a vital part of her healing process. Nori has been a Unitarian Universalist minister for thirty-two years. *(pp. 34, 41, 92, 139, 162)*

I. Sandz wrote her poem, *Instructions for Letting Go*, after the unexpected death on January 1, 2021 of a neighbor who was a close friend. She was devastated. When her friend died, about a hundred people gathered, masked and socially distanced, in front of his house to honor him. She says the title is ironic—she wishes that someone could have given her instructions for grieving. *(p. 104)*

Pauline K. Schmookler was in theater much of her life, and wrote several plays that were produced at universities around the country. After her husband died in 1967, she turned to poetry because it was the only form through which she could express her grief effectively. Pauline's poetry was published in *Identity*, *Unknowns* and other magazines. She passed away in 2002. *(pp. 18, 118, 132, 180)*

Mara Teitel Sheade always wanted to be a writer, but she rarely wrote creatively until after her brother's death from cancer in 1989. As her love of writing grew, she found meaning and sadness in the knowledge that her brother's death was the beginning of something that means so much to her now. She has since led writing workshops in schools, libraries, and senior centers that focus on writing as a tool for healing. You can read more about how her brother's death changed her in the "Time Passes" section of this book. *(pp. 1, 107, 170, 204, 206, 207)*

Fereshteh Sholevar was her mother's loving caregiver for three years. Seven years after her mother's death, Fereshteh still grieves, but she feels her mother watching over her in the forms of the birds and flowers that her mother loved. Fereshteh is Iranian-American writer and poet who came to the USA in 1978. She writes in 4 languages and has authored 8 books of poetry, a children's book, and a novel. *Pebbles of Sorrow* is the sixth poem she has dedicated to her mother. *(p. 157)*

Robin Lahargoue Shorett was twelve when her eighteen-year-old brother Michael died in an alcohol-related car accident. Robin was a prolific writer as a child and her mother contacted me about participating in the first edition of this book. Now forty years old and a mother of two, Robin looks back on losing her brother in the "Time Passes" section of this book. *(pp. 160, 234)*

Elizabeth Léonie Simpson was a developmental psychologist who wrote extensively in her field. She was a contributor to the first edition of this book and was working on a book about memory at that time. Elizabeth also published two novels, a novella, and numerous other works of non-fiction. Her poem was written for her daughter, who died in 1986 from Hodgkin's Disease. Elizabeth died in 2019 at the age of ninety-five. *(p. 188)*

Ken Slesarik found his twenty-four-year-old son Kenny at home, dead from an accidental drug overdose in 2019. His grief was so profound that it almost drove him to suicide, which was prevented only when he clearly heard Kenny's voice say, "Please don't hurt yourself." Ken is a special education teacher who has also provided professional development for teachers, spoken at conferences, and written poetry curricula. Ken says his mission now is "to empower those who grieve, through the healing power of poetry." *(pp. 24, 144)*

Julie D. Strongson-Aldape wrote *Plastic-Covered Phone* about her father and stepmother. Her grief in losing them to Covid has been made more difficult because of the lack of the usual rituals around death and mourning during the pandemic. Julie has a PhD in Comparative Literature and is an English instructor at a military academy prep school. She does most of her writing, especially poetry, when she is working through personal struggles. *(p. 64)*

Shirley Thacker met her friend Tom Dorton over fifty years ago in high school, when she was a freshman and he was a senior. Beloved by the community, Tom spent sixty days in the ICU struggling with Covid before he finally succumbed. His wife was not allowed to visit until the minutes before he died, and even then, only one of their three children were permitted to join her. Shirley taught K-2 for forty-two years and was a teacher consultant for the Indiana Writing Project. She now volunteers two hours each day to help struggling young readers. *(p. 80)*

Lucy Trevitt wrote her poem in response to the tragic death of a young friend, but she has also dealt with a number of deaths herself. An artist and a poet, Lucy has lived with significant illness and disability for most of her life. She says, "my creative process accompanies me as a necessity; it is the alchemy for navigating my life, and enables me to transform my experiences into their essence, and their healing." *(p. 145)*

Yvonne Ugarte discovered, while working as a nursing assistant in hospice, that many patients just wanted her to sit with them. She often held their hands in their last moments. *Bill* was written for the multitude of nurses who have done that during the pandemic. Yvonne's son Emil died twenty-three years ago after two bouts of meningitis, just before turning two. She has been writing poetry since she was five. Known locally as an environmental poet, Yvonne was thrilled to perform one of her poems for over three hundred people at a climate change rally in 2019. *(p. 87)*

Terry Ray Van Huss wrote his poem, *The Disclaimer*, for his friend Todd, who died at age twenty-seven from an allergic reaction to an allergy shot that he had been getting regularly since he was a child. Terry is an Information Technology manager as well as a proud father and grandfather who enjoys painting, photography, and occasionally, writing poetry. *(p. 179)*

Margaret Wadsworth's mother was in a memory-care facility when the pandemic hit. When the family could no longer visit and her mother's health deteriorated, they arranged for home hospice care.

However, her mother died the day before she was to come home. Margaret is a family physician who has loved poetry since she was a child. She finds that writing poems can transmute her pain in a simple, elegant way. *(p. 45)*

Norman Wendth's poem *Thoughts While on Hold to the Florist* was written while feeling overwhelmed after multiple deaths. He had been grieving the loss of his father when, a few months later, his aunt died. His wife's grandmother died, just days after his aunt. Struggling with those losses, he found himself again grieving the death of his baby sister over thirty years earlier. Now retired, Norman was a professor of literature when the first edition of this book was published. *(p. 99)*

Penelope Kellogg Winkler was very close to her grandmother, who died one night at the age of ninety. She had been planning to visit her but procrastinated, and as a result, never got the chance to say goodbye. Penelope is married and has a daughter whom she named after her grandmother. *(p. 178)* *

Nickie Zavinsky created *No!* to express how she felt after her mother's death in 1989. She has found that painting and drawing have been very healing during the difficult times in her life; sometimes, even just coloring in a coloring book has been helpful. *(p. 33)*

Courage to Write

*"Poetry is a natural medicine; it is like a homeopathic tincture derived from the stuff of life itself—**your experience**...Poems speak to us when nothing else will. Poetry helps us to **feel** our lives rather than just be numb. The page, touched with our poem, becomes a place for painful feelings to be held, explored, and transformed."*

John Fox, from *Poetic Medicine*

I invite you to join the contributors to this book in expressing your own grief, for yourself, through poem-making. The next ten pages are blank, reserved for *your* voice, for your own poems or writing.

The contributors to this book found validation, insight and healing in expressing their experience through poetry. "I carried the grief of losing my daughter for twenty years until [I wrote] about it. Gradually in the writing, the healing process began," said one.

If you've never written poetry, you may not know where to begin. Here's a suggestion: pick a poem in this book that moves you, and choose a line from that poem. Begin your poem with that line. What do you feel when you read that line and poem? What does it remind you of in your own loss? Are there sounds, smells, images, or memories that arise? Write those down.

Your poem could be the remembrance of an everyday experience, something now lost that you once cherished or took for granted. It might mirror the depths of your love, or reveal thoughts or feelings that frighten you: even anger at your loved one, or a loss of faith in God. It's all OK. Write it all down. We can't heal if we are afraid to tend to our wounds.

You may think you can't write, that your words aren't good enough. But I assure you, they are precious, worth more than anything else in this book because they speak *your* truth. Your poem doesn't have to be pretty. Not everyone in this book used beautiful language. Write what's true for you. Nothing else matters.

About John Fox and the
Institute for Poetic Medicine

The Institute for Poetic Medicine (IPM) was founded in 2005 by John Fox, Practitioner of Poetic Medicine (PPM). Before its founding, since 1981, John had practiced poetry-as-healer nationally and internationally. He is the author of *Poetic Medicine: The Healing Art of Poem-Making* and *Finding What You Didn't Lose: Expressing Your Creativity and Truth Through Poem-Making*. His work is featured in the PBS documentary *Healing Words: Poetry and Medicine*.

IPM's mission is: *To awaken soulfulness in the human voice*. IPM offers tools and support to heal body, mind, heart and spirit through the creative and therapeutic process of hearing, speaking/sharing and writing poetry. It is dedicated to funding projects that serve people at the so-called margins. IPM provides a three-year, master's level training program. It provides deep resources and active support to helping professionals in education, medicine, psychology, pastoral care, cancer and grief support, among others.

To learn more about the Institute for Poetic Medicine and whom they serve, visit https://poeticmedicine.org.

About the Editor

Mike Bernhardt is an award-winning writer whose work has appeared in many print and online publications. He grew up in New York City, where he wrote poetry and kept a journal throughout his teenage years. He moved to the San Francisco Bay Area when he was nineteen and was working as an electrician when he met his first wife, Susan, in 1983.

In the years after Susan's death in 1991, Mike met and married his second wife, Yvonne, and published the first edition of *Voices of the Grieving Heart*. He retired in 2016 from a career in information technology and began writing again. Mike and Yvonne raised a son and still live in the Bay Area, where they currently live with their two cats.

Visit Mike's website at https://mikebernhardt.net.

If this book inspired you or if you found it helpful, please consider leaving a positive review on Amazon and Goodreads.

Profits from the sale of this book are going to the Institute for Poetic Medicine, a non-profit 501(c) (3) charitable organization.

Made in the USA
Las Vegas, NV
07 April 2021